JOURNEY WITHIN

DYNAMICS OF SHADOW WORK
"The Blueprint"

An Illuminated Step-by-Step Path to Your Inner Landscape
Book and Integration Blueprint by

KING GAIA

Copyright © 2025 King Gaia

All rights reserved. No part of this book, in any format—including but not limited to print, digital, audio, online e-courses, embodiment tools, coaching sessions and merchandise—may be copied, reproduced, stored, or transmitted by any means, whether electronic, mechanical, photocopying, recording, or otherwise, without prior written permission from the publisher. The only exception is brief quotations used in reviews or critical discussions, as permitted by copyright law.

Published and printed by King Gaia in the United States of America.

First Edition/First Printing, 2025

ISBN 979-8-9926942-1-5

For inquiries, collaboration requests or additional resources, visit:

www.KingGaia.com

DEDICATION

For my son—

You are my greatest masterpiece, my most profound lesson, the greatest reward, and my deepest love. Watching you grow, dream, and become is the purest joy of my life. You are the reason I strive, the reason I heal, the reason I dare to be my fullest self.

May you always walk bold in your truth, stand in your power, and know that you are infinitely loved— not just for what you do, but for who you are. No matter where life takes you, my heart beats with yours, always and forever.

With all my love,
Mom

You've been summoned by the light within you.

Dear Reader,

At the edges of awareness, where light meets shadow, a quiet call beckons. It is the voice of the unseen, the forgotten—the parts of ourselves we've tucked away in silence. This is where the journey begins—not outward, but inward—to the hidden corridors of the soul that whisper for recognition in the dark.

Shadow work invites us beneath the surface of our being, into the caverns of the self—innermost spaces long neglected or misunderstood. Here lie the fragments of ourselves we've feared or wished away. Yet, these shadows are not adversaries to be vanquished; they are lost children of the psyche, yearning for recognition, compassion, and love.

As we turn inward, shedding layers, we uncover aspects of ourselves calling for understanding and integration. Life's hardships can scatter the soul, leaving us fragmented. Reclaiming these lost pieces is essential to becoming whole. But how do we recognize or reclaim what we don't even know exists? How do we embrace what we were taught to fear?

This is the essence of shadow work—a courageous, ongoing process of self-exploration, balance, and acceptance. Within these pages, you will find research, stories, reflections, and practices to guide you toward reunion with your truest self—embracing both light and shadow. It is not darkness that wounds us, but our refusal to face it. Denial or avoidance only perpetuates emptiness and suffering; acknowledgment is the path to liberation.

This book is an invitation to witness and welcome the unseen, to embrace every facet of your being: light and shadow, surface and depth, fear and love. Within the shadow lies not just the root of our wounds but the seed of our awakening.

By opening these pages with intention, you are choosing a path of radical self-love, authentic-self cultivation, limitless-self activation, and self-mastery. This is not an easy path—but for those willing to step into their deepest power, it holds the promise of transformation, healing, and profound liberation.

As your personal shadow guide, I will help you understand and navigate the path inward, clarify your intent, and direct your efforts with confidence. While I will share elements of my own journey, this book is not about my experiences. Instead, I will highlight the key turning points and lessons that have shaped me into the ever-healing, always-learning shadow work expert I am today.

My transparency, vulnerability, and ongoing transformation will serve as a lantern to illuminate your path. I am deeply honored to take on this assignment. Through my challenges and self-exploration, I have come to understand that true healing and growth are not found in perfection, but in embracing our humanity and the intricacies of the human condition.

The shadow is not a place of peril but a realm of profound potential. It holds the keys to your unclaimed gifts and untapped strength. By venturing into the shadow, you will emerge into a light of your own making—brighter, truer, and more powerful for having dared to look within.

With this understanding, I hope my journey serves as a beacon for yours. Through suffering, self-exploration, and the transformative power of shadow work, I rose above self-sabotage, self-doubt, and the gripping darkness that once held me back—and so can you. My humanity, imperfections, and resilience are proof that healing and transformation are within reach for us all. I see your power, your strength, and your capacity to rise. No matter the obstacles, you too can transcend.

This journey is neither of light nor darkness, but of wholeness—a reunion with the full spectrum of your humanity. Let these stories, reflections, and practices be your companions, guiding you toward a homecoming with your truest self.

So, dear reader, what awaits you in the depths of your being?

May these illuminated pages serve you well.

Let the journey begin.

ABOUT JOURNEY WITHIN

Journey Within is a sacred path of illumination, deep self-exploration, transformation, and inner mastery. It is the process of peeling back layers of conditioning, fears, and limitations to reconnect with the essence of one's true self. This journey is both personal and collective—a continuous unfolding of self-awareness, healing, and alignment with divine purpose, rooted in radical self-love, authenticity, and spiritual evolution.

Journey Within Ecosystem

Framework

- **Essentials Digest (eBook/Audio Book)** — A concise introduction to the fundamentals of shadow work, laying the groundwork for deep self-exploration.
- **The Blueprint (Print Book + eCourse)** — A powerful combination that connects and interprets shadow work fundamentals and processes throughout The Journey Within, guiding you step by step toward individuation—the path to becoming your most authentic and whole self.
  - **Print Book** — Explores the philosophy, core concepts, and sacred dynamics of inner work, unveiling the path inward one doorway at a time. Includes the highly sought-after **Know Thyself Self-Discovery Shadow Work Kit**, featuring 111 introspective prompts designed to help you unveil your shadow, navigate the unknown, and deepen self-love.

- **eCourse** – Expands on each chapter with in-depth lectures, exercises, actionable steps and an interactive, step-by-step map for deeper integration. This map, laying out your very own **Path to Individuation**, moves beyond theory into real-life application, featuring threshold checkpoints and engaging integration pause spreads to assess progress, align energy, and confirm what's naturally unfolding in your journey. **Access the Journey Within Blueprint e-Course URL/QR Code on Page 10.**

The Tools of Embodiment

- **The Lantern Tarot Oracle:** A 130-cards minimalist introspective deck designed for deep healing and shadow work.
- **Sanctuary** 7-Day Conscious Detachment Ritual (Aura Detox, Chakra Clearing and Cord Cutting)
- **Majesty Candle:** A 7-knob cord-cutting candle that connects to the energy work of the process.
- **Anchor** Grounding and Protective Jewelry

Sustainable Practice and Ongoing Support

- **One Vessel Membership:** Weekly Spiritual Life Coaching & Guided Shadow Work

"Thank you for your support and for the opportunity to be of service to you!"

King Gaia
(she/her)

ABOUT THIS BOOK

Hello and welcome! I am so glad your intuition led you here.

Let's get straight to it—self-awareness and self-care aren't just practices; they're profound gifts. Shadow work is the key to unlocking your highest potential, embracing your true self, and identifying what—obvious or hidden—is holding you back from elevating your soul and manifesting the life of your dreams.

This book was divinely channeled, mindfully vetted, and intentionally crafted to simplify the mystery and complexity of shadow work. As part of *The Journey Within* framework, this book serves as your official blueprint—guiding you from who and where you are now to your most authentic, limitless, purpose-aligned, and self-empowered version.

These pages aim to demystify shadow work and make it relatable, accessible, and practical. This is more than a book—it's a mindset shift, a deep preparation, and a transformational guide. Shadow work should feel natural, rewarding, vital, and profoundly healing.

What to Expect

Shadow work is a **journey**, not a one-time event. This book is designed to fully support you and guide you through this transformational process in three key ways:

- **Understanding the Foundations** — Learning the core principles of shadow work.
- **Experiencing the Journey Within** — Contemplating, feeling, and exploring your inner world.
- **Taking Inspired Action** — Integrating and embodying the work in your daily life.

To ensure a **clear, structured, and practical** approach, this book is structured into five key chapters to guide you through every stage of your shadow work journey:

- **Concepts** — The foundation of shadow work: what it is, why it matters, purpose and benefits, and how it unfolds. Everything you need to know to provide clarity and facilitate the process.
- **Dynamics** — The underlying forces shaping and influencing your 'light vs shadow' experience.
- **Preparation** — Setting clear intentions, cultivating the right mindset, and establishing deep significance for an effective shadow work journey.
- **Application** — Starting and navigating your journey within. Exploring shadow work approaches, navigating the shadow self, and engaging with tools and techniques for long-lasting transformation.
- **Integration** — Embodying your breakthroughs, sustaining healing and growth, and weaving shadow work into your daily life.

Shadow work isn't just about uncovering and healing—it's about **becoming.**

JOURNEY WITHIN: DYNAMICS OF SHADOW WORK

Each chapter builds upon the last, offering a structured yet flexible roadmap for your shadow work journey. Move at your own pace, engage deeply, trust your process, and allow your transformation to unfold.

Along with research, stories, reflections, and practices, throughout these chapters, you'll experience integration tools to help you embody this work in daily life.

- **Know Thyself Self-Discovery Shadow Work Kit**, featuring a collection 111 thought-provoking introspective prompts designed to help you unveil your shadow, navigate the unknown, and deepen self-love.

- The **Journey Within Blueprint,** a structured companion *online course* expanding on each chapter with in-depth lectures, exercises, actionable steps and an interactive, step-by-step map for deeper integration. This map, laying out your very own **Path to Individuation**, moves beyond theory into real-life application, featuring threshold checkpoints and engaging integration pause spreads to assess progress, align energy, and confirm what's naturally unfolding in your journey.

This book and the blueprint are inseparable—one lays the foundation, while the other guides you in applying and embodying the knowledge. Shadow work isn't just something you learn—it's something you experience. And I'm here for you every step of the way!

How to Make the Most of This Book

- **Engage Fully:** Read actively, reflect deeply, and use the exercises provided. This book is a working text, not a passive read.

- **Go at Your Own Pace:** Some sections will feel light, others intense. Honor your process. There is no rush. Trust yourself. Trust the Process.

- **Use This as a Companion, Not a Rulebook:** Nothing is written on stone. We are all navigating our very own unique journeys. Adapt what resonates and make this journey your own.

- **Seek Support When Needed:** Shadow work can unearth deep emotions. Reach out to trusted resources—coaches, therapists, community support, or spiritual guides. You are not meant to do this alone.

Available Resources for Support & Integration

Shadow work is not meant to be done in isolation. To help you deepen your practice, additional resources are available within our community and offerings.

- **Journey Within: Integration Circle** *(6-Week Integration Cohort)* A guided immersion and focused study group exploring the Journey Within doorways – and how to map this sacred shadow work onto your unique inner landscape and real-life circumstances.

- **Shadow Self: The Sacred Unknown** — In-depth shadow-self masterclass
- **Guided 1:1 Shadow Work Sessions** — Personalized deep dives with tailored guidance.
- **Weekly Group Shadow Work Coaching** — One Vessel membership offering an ongoing supportive, community-driven space for shared experiences and accountability.
- **The Lantern Tarot Oracle** — A special deck designed for self-inquiry and subconscious exploration.
- **Shadow Work Kits** — Mindfully curated journal prompts for self-reflection.
- **Sanctuary Conscious Detachment Ritual** — A guided practice for release and renewal.
- **Majesty Candle** — A ritual tool for cord-cutting, intention-setting, and energy work.
- **Grounding & Protection Jewelry** — Wearable tools for energetic support.

These resources exist to support you beyond these pages, providing continuity and a container for your evolution. Shadow work is a journey, and you don't have to walk it alone. Please visit our website https://www.kinggaia.com for upcoming events, training and reservations.

Here, Now and Next

Before we get started, take a moment to acknowledge yourself. Right here, right now, you are exactly where you need to be—physically, mentally, emotionally, and energetically. You are showing up for yourself as a mindful co-creator, ready to master your energy and transform your life.

The Journey Within Blueprint is your key to applying the insights from this book through interactive guidance, embodiment exercises, and deeper practices. **This is how you make it happen.**

THE BLUEPRINT

Ready to dive in? Scan the QR code or visit https://blueprint.kinggaia.com to get started. Everything you need is already waiting for you. See you there!

E-COURSE LECTURE: "Welcome! You Are Here"

CONTENTS

About Journey Within 1
About this Book 4
Prologue 13
Introduction: Self-Love is Why 18

CHAPTER 1: CONCEPTS 27

Section 1. Definition 28
Section 2. Origin 32
Section 3. Philosophy 34
Section 4. Principles 37
Section 5. Purpose and Benefits 40
Section 6. Common Misconceptions 44

CHAPTER 2: DYNAMICS 75

Section 7. Awareness 76
Section 8. Realization 81
Section 9. Forces at Work 84
Section 10. Soul Whispers 91
Section 11. Divine Intervention 97
Section 12. A 'Tower Moment' 99
Section 13. Dark Night of the Soul 101

CHAPTER 3: PREPARATION 125

Section 14. Significance 128
Section 15. Openness and Readiness to Heal 133
Section 16. Setting Clear Intentions 137

CHAPTER 4: APPLICATION 161

Section 17. Approaches 164
Section 18. Unveiling Your Shadow Self................................ 165
Section 19. Understanding/Accepting the Shadow Self... 170
Section 20. Our Shadow Profile..175
Section 21. Working with the Shadow Self......................... 183
Section 22. The Alchemy Process...................................... 228

CHAPTER 5: INTEGRATION 259

Section 23. How to Navigate and Sustain Your Journey ... 264
Section 24. Anchoring Yourself 268
Section 25. Unlocking Your Soul's Purpose (Akasha)........... 301
Section 26. The Ultimate Outcome 313

Afterword 318
Acknowledgements... 321
Meet the Author 323

Journey Within Doorways

01. The Bench 50
02. The Sanctuary 115
03. The Lantern 146
04. The Compass 148
05. The Cloak 150
06. The Grotto 191
07. The Dagger 221
08. The Bridge 271
09. The Path 278
10. The Summit 281
11. The Vessel 291

PROLOGUE

THE THING ABOUT SELF-CARE

Self-Care is Not Selfish

Self-care is a significant topic because, despite its commercialization, it remains complex and challenging for many to embrace. Now, more than ever, prioritizing self-care is essential as we navigate a world that glorifies multitasking, burnout culture, personal disregard, and self-sacrifice.

In 2021, after the pandemic's big wave, I organized my first online conference. Hosting a live expo wasn't yet feasible, but I wanted to provide immediate post-pandemic healing and support to our community. "Online" was the fastest way to deliver. Looking back, that small project was the seed for our Journey Within framework.

As part of the program, I included an onboarding questionnaire with a priority survey to understand participants' needs and better support them. One response stood out. A student wrote:

"Thank you for the survey, but I don't want any self-help right now. I just want to help others. Can you help me with that?"

I had mixed feelings reading that. I knew she meant every word. The empath in me felt touched and related deeply. But the healer, teacher, and shadow work coach in me felt heartbroken. I understood the high cost of her self-sacrificing approach—she was eager to dismiss her own struggles just to prioritize others. She felt as any self-help or self-care effort towards her benefit was a 'selfish ask'—a luxury or priority she didn't deserve while others needed her.

I was reminded of the sign inside airplanes: "Put on your own oxygen mask first before assisting others." You help others by helping yourself and filling your cup. You simply can't help anyone if you are sick, scattered, empty, overwhelmed, unfulfilled, compromised, or depleted.

The Cost of Self-Neglect

The price of self-sacrifice is too high. Many of us believe it is necessary or for "the greater good," but self-neglect helps no one—not even those we try to support. When you constantly put yourself last, you send a message—to yourself and the universe—that you are not a priority, not important, not worthy. You also teach others how to treat you: with disregard. Your self-neglect declares that you have no significance and your needs are not to be considered.

We cannot and will not find balance, true love, happiness, or fulfillment if we abandon and betray ourselves. The universe has a way of forcing us to listen, whether through a humbling message or a rude awakening. Self-neglect will catch up with you. I know. I've been there.

I was so focused on doing, doing, and more doing—staying busy, distracting myself from deeper issues, and ignoring red flags—until I hit a wall. Until I ended up in a hospital bed, forced to reconsider my priorities. The universe said, "No more." And divine intervention was served.

We must listen to our bodies, trust our intuition, and recognize the signs. The universe is always in constant communication with us, guiding us toward self-awareness, self-care, and self-love.

Self-Care is the Foundation of Self-Empowerment

We need to remove the stigma, shame, and guilt surrounding self-care. Self-care is not selfish. There is a difference between being selfish and being self-centered.

Being self-centered in a soul-focused way means prioritizing your well-being so you can show up fully for yourself and others. You cannot pour from an empty cup. You are meant to help others from your overflow, not by depleting yourself.

Self-care is not a one-time event—it's an ongoing practice. It's not just about bubble baths, spas, or brunch dates. True self-care includes listening to and attending our needs:

- ✔ Eating well and staying hydrated
- ✔ Making time for self-reflection
- ✔ Prioritizing rest and sleep
- ✔ Taking breaks, vacations, or staycations
- ✔ Spending time in nature
- ✔ Turning off your phone for a day
- ✔ Keeping up with medical appointments
- ✔ Honoring your boundaries

JOURNEY WITHIN: DYNAMICS OF SHADOW WORK

- ✔ And most importantly, doing your shadow work–addressing deep wounds, unprocessed events, and untreated traumas

If you don't take care of yourself, who will? If you don't love, value, and respect yourself, why would anyone else?

Self-care is not a luxury or a special appointment; it's a necessity. It ensures that you have the energy, stability, and strength to navigate life, pursue your dreams, and show up for the people who matter. **Self-care is how you take your power back.**

When you prioritize self-care, you reclaim your essence, expand your radiance, and elevate your vibration. In doing so, you invite miracles, blessings, aligned connections, and true love into your life. Self-care is simply non-negotiable.

E-COURSE LECTURE: "Expressions of Self-Care"

Know Thyself: Introspections 001-002

1. What is your stand on self-care?
2. Do you have a self-care routine? If so, what does it look like?

INTRODUCTION

SELF-LOVE IS WHY

Before we explore shadow work—what it is, what it isn't, and why it matters—the first thing you need to know is this: **shadow work is a profound, compassionate, and assertive act of self-love.**

We can't talk about the what or the how of shadow work without first addressing the why. Why would you want to embrace shadow work?

Self-love is why.

What is Self-Love?

Self-love is unconditional acceptance, deep appreciation, and intentional nurturing of oneself. It means recognizing your intrinsic worth, treating yourself with compassion and respect, and embracing every aspect of who you are—including your human condition, vulnerabilities, weaknesses, and past mistakes.

Self-love shows up as:

Inner Acceptance & Compassion

- Loving yourself deeply and unconditionally, without relying on external validation.

- Embracing yourself fully—flaws, mistakes, and imperfections included—without judgment.
- Offering yourself the same kindness and care that you would give a loved one, especially in difficult moments.

Emotional & Mental Well-being

- Allowing yourself to feel and express emotions instead of suppressing them.
- Seeking support when needed and engaging in activities that bring joy, peace, and relaxation.
- Practicing mindfulness, meditation, and self-reflection to stay connected to your inner self.

Boundaries & Alignment

- Setting and maintaining healthy boundaries to protect your well-being.
- Honoring your needs, desires, and goals rather than being overly influenced by external pressures.
- Living in alignment with your values and principles, making choices that reflect your true self.

Growth & Empowerment

- Cultivating self-confidence and trusting yourself to handle life's challenges.

- Committing to personal development and continuous learning.
- Celebrating your achievements—big or small—and acknowledging your progress.

Now, on the other side of the coin...
Lack of self-love —that one gets messy.

How Does a Lack of Self-Love Show Up in Our Lives?

When we struggle with self-love, it affects every aspect of our lives. It shapes the way we think, the choices we make, and the relationships we build. Some common ways a lack of self-love manifests include:

- **People-pleasing:** Prioritizing others' needs over your own to feel worthy or accepted.
- **Self-sabotage:** Avoiding success, love, or happiness because deep down, you don't believe you deserve it.
- **Over-apologizing:** Feeling responsible for things that aren't your fault and constantly seeking external approval.
- **Harsh self-criticism:** Engaging in negative self-talk and believing you are never "good enough."
- **Tolerating toxic relationships:** Staying in harmful or unbalanced relationships out of fear of being alone.
- **Fear of failure or rejection:** Avoiding risks or new opportunities due to a deep-seated belief that you are destined to fail.

- **Neglecting self-care:** Feeling guilty for taking care of yourself, seeing it as selfish rather than necessary.

These struggles stem from deeply ingrained beliefs of unworthiness, rooted in shame, guilt, and fear. We've been conditioned to prioritize external validation, avoid discomfort, and downplay our needs. Breaking free from this conditioning requires unlearning, healing, and transformation.

Why Do We Struggle with Self-Love?

Self-love feels difficult because we've been conditioned to believe we are unworthy. Shame, guilt, and fear are programmed into us through social conditioning, negative self-talk, and misunderstandings of love. These false paradigms keep us stuck in cycles of self-doubt, self-sacrifice, and emotional neglect.

Overcoming these struggles requires self-awareness, self-compassion, and intentional healing. Through shadow work, we reframe limiting beliefs, confront internalized fears, and reclaim our inherent worth. Practices like journaling, meditation, and professional guidance can facilitate this journey toward self-acceptance.

What Self-Love is NOT

Self-love is not selfishness, narcissism, indulgence, perfectionism, avoidance, isolation, or toxic positivity. It is not about ignoring problems, suppressing emotions, or striving for unattainable self-sufficiency.

Instead, self-love is about balance. It is about honoring your needs, creating space for healing, and fostering healthy, fulfilling relationships—with yourself and others.

Self-Love Through Shadow Work

Every aspect of self-love requires knowing and accepting all parts of yourself. Shadow work is an act of self-love because it:

- Embraces your whole self—the light and the shadow.
- Heals and transforms wounds instead of allowing them to fester.
- Empowers you to make aligned choices based on self-awareness.
- Fosters compassion for yourself and others.
- Helps you create healthy boundaries and reclaim your power.
- Nurtures radical self-love by confronting and healing deep-rooted fears and limiting beliefs.

Your Invitation to Self-Love

I personally struggled with self-love big time, and for me, it often showed up as procrastination. I would stay busy—doing all the little things that didn't truly matter—just to avoid facing the things that actually needed my attention. I convinced myself I was being productive, but deep down, I was just distracting myself from my own growth. The

INTRODUCTION

things that could elevate me, expand me, or challenge me? I'd push them aside. Not because I was lazy, but because a part of me questioned whether I was truly worthy of success, fulfillment, and ease.

Shadow work exposed those hidden fears and limiting beliefs. It forced me to confront the ways I was playing small, doubting myself, and avoiding my own power. The more I peeled back the layers, the more I saw how much of my life was shaped by unconscious programming—fear of failure, fear of rejection, fear of being seen, even fear of my own brilliance.

But through this journey, I found something greater than fear: my personal power.

As I embraced radical self-love, I started making real changes in my life—not just in my mindset, but in my actions.

- I began nourishing my body with healthy food, movement, and rest, understanding that my physical well-being was just as sacred as my spiritual journey.
- I gave myself permission to be vulnerable and authentic in my relationships, no longer shrinking, wearing masks, people-pleasing, or dimming my light for anyone.
- I committed to letting go of past mistakes and practicing self-forgiveness, recognizing that every misstep was a lesson, not a life sentence. I learn to love that I am a perfectly imperfect human being.

- I stopped waiting for external validation and started honoring myself. I stopped procrastinating on my purpose and started walking boldly in it.

That ignited my light and I decided to embody radiance. Self-love is not something we "earn"—it's something we choose. And every day, I choose me.

I want you to experience your personal power and inner radiance too. Accept this as an invitation to practice self-love. Your self-love journey begins exactly where you are, as you are. No need for perfection—just willingness. Shadow work is your gateway to healing, empowerment, and radical self-love.

By facing your shadows, you reclaim your power. By embracing self-love, you transform your life.

E-COURSE LECTURE: "Self-Love vs Radical Self-Love"

* Know Thyself : Introspections 003-008*

3. What is your interpretation of self-love?

4. Do you find yourself struggling with self-love?

5. What aspects of self-love feel unnatural, forced, or uncomfortable to you?

6. What would you like self-love to look like in your life?

7. How do you presently show up for yourself?

8. What can be improved in the way you show up for yourself?

CHAPTER ONE
CONCEPTS

SECTION 1. DEFINITION

The simplest way to describe shadow work is self-contemplation. We all have conscious and subconscious aspects of ourselves. Consciousness is the light, and subconsciousness is the shadow.

Shadow work is the process of exploring and integrating the subconscious aspects of ourselves that have been repressed, denied, or left unresolved.

It's important to acknowledge that the word "shadow" may invite misinterpretation, stigma, or confusion. There is a tendency to assume or label something as "wrong," "dark," or "evil" when we don't know how to interpret it or process it out of ignorance or its nuance.

The term "shadow" is used because these aspects haven't been illuminated by our consciousness. We have chosen, consciously or subconsciously, to keep them hidden as a defense or coping mechanism, keeping us safe and protecting us from the pain or uncertainty of whatever circumstances created the shadow because we didn't know how to handle it at the time.

A shadow is a subconscious aspect of ourselves that we don't see, recognize, acknowledge, or accept. A shadow is not darkness alone. Just like our physical shadow needs sunlight to appear, so do our non-physical ones.

As part of our human condition, we often keep unique experiences, feelings, emotions, and reactions to trauma or shock tucked away, either deliberately or completely unaware of it, because it was easier than dealing with it at the moment or we just didn't know how.

CONCEPTS

Shadows are a blessing in disguise; they show us where love is absent, like breadcrumbs for us to follow. If we choose to follow, they help us identify and leave behind emptiness, pain, anxiety, sorrow, conflict, wounds, restlessness, nightmares, and suffering.

Shadows form when an experience—whether ours or another's reaction to us—is suppressed due to pain, fear, or uncertainty. We suppressed it or 'archived' it away—most likely subconsciously—out of survival or as a coping mechanism, because the experience or their reaction to us was assumed to be bad, evil, painful, scary, confusing, shocking or wrong.

Not every experience in our lives becomes a shadow, but as long as we are alive, even the smallest and most insignificant events can trigger or project a shadow that has been neglected.

Imagine you experienced heartache, great shame, or disappointment at some point in your life. You were navigating life the best you could, writing the pages of your book of life, and experiencing your "hero's journey." When it happened, you didn't know how to face it or deal with it because it was too much to handle or you were too young to know how to handle it, so your brain, heart, or soul did the best it could to keep you safe and placed a temporary bookmark or flag to help you move on. But that bookmark or flag created a dent or a hole in your character, in your sense of self, in your perception of life, and you may or may not be aware of it.

Eventually, shadows will emerge for us to take care of, manifesting as mental, emotional, spiritual, and even

JOURNEY WITHIN: DYNAMICS OF SHADOW WORK

physical issues. They show up as blockages and interferences that need to be resolved. They affect our energy, authenticity, relationships, money, careers, creativity, paradigms, and manifestation processes. This is when prioritizing shadow work becomes urgent. If we choose not to do shadow work, life becomes dull, challenging, confusing, empty, meaningless, and overwhelming.

At some point, the bookmark in our book of life becomes obvious, and we need to go back and revisit it to finish that chapter, close the cycle, and get closure. That's healing, personal transformation, and self-care. That's shadow work.

When we go within to do our inner work, that process is called shadow work. Emphasis on work. Inner work! It's not easy, and it does not happen overnight. Shadow work is a process of exploring and integrating the parts of ourselves that we have repressed or denied, often referred to as our "shadow." These parts can include negative emotions, unconscious beliefs, past traumas, and aspects of our personality that we consider undesirable or unacceptable.

The shadow doesn't want to stay in the dark; it wants light and acknowledgement. It wants us to become aware of it so we can deal with it, heal, tap into our authentic energy, grow, manifest our best life, and evolve. We owe it to ourselves to resolve pending issues and transcend them. We can make a conscious decision to work on ourselves, or we may manifest divine intervention we can no longer ignore.

Visualize shadow work like this: Imagine our subconscious is a cave—a dark cave. We don't know what's in there, but it's affecting many or all aspects of our lives. At some point, we feel the need for a reset or a change of perspective. We become aware of our narratives, recognizing loops and patterns, knowing we deserve better and there is more to life than lack and struggles. So we decide to explore, getting ourselves a flashlight to illuminate the cave. When the flashlight (a metaphor for our consciousness) points at the darkness (a metaphor for our subconsciousness), it illuminates the issue, allowing us to acknowledge it and do something about it—heal it, challenge it, integrate it, work it out, remove it—whatever feels right. The "shadow" disappears with illumination; it's revealed and it is no longer an issue. It becomes a work in progress that we are taking care of or a mission accomplished.

Shadow work changes our lives forever, personally, professionally, socially, and in every aspect—our energy, physical body, emotional, spiritual, mental, and financial well-being. It involves going within, exploring our inner landscape layer by layer, addressing pain and trauma, old programming, social conditioning, self-sabotage, ego stereotypes, and dark archetypes.

SECTION 2. ORIGIN

Shadow work origin is not metaphysical. It's psychological. The shadow concept was first brought into the Western world by Swiss psychologist Carl Jung (1875-1961). Jung was a prominent psychiatrist and psychoanalyst who founded analytical psychology. His work expanded on Sigmund Freud's theories of the unconscious mind.

He described it as the unconscious and disowned parts of our personalities that the ego fails to see, acknowledge, and accept. It is any aspect of ourselves that is not exposed to the light of our consciousness. But is very present, subtle or not, like a shadow following our every step.

He introduced the concept of the "shadow" as part of his analytical psychology, which explores the unconscious aspects of the human psyche: the ego (conscious mind), the personal unconscious (individual experiences and memories), and the collective unconscious (shared, universal archetypes).

Shadow work involves bringing these hidden aspects of the self into conscious awareness, accepting them without judgment, and integrating them into our sense of identity. It is a process of shining light into the darkness of the psyche, embracing all facets of our being – both light and shadow – with compassion and understanding.

Jung argued that the shadow is not inherently negative; and he emphasized the importance of acknowledging and integrating the shadow into the conscious self. This process, known as individuation, leads to a more balanced and whole personality.

While Jung's work laid the foundation, shadow work has expanded beyond psychology into metaphysics, spirituality, and personal development as a holistic tool for self-discovery and transformation.

SECTION 3. PHILOSOPHY

Shadow work is the sacred art of self-integration, a transformative journey that brings the unconscious into the light of awareness. Rooted in Jungian psychology, shadow work is based on the understanding that every human being has a shadow self—the hidden, suppressed, or denied aspects of our personality.

At its core, shadow work is not about eliminating darkness but embracing wholeness. It operates under the philosophy that true self-mastery requires integrating all parts of ourselves—the light and the dark, the known and the unknown. Without this integration, we remain fragmented, trapped in unconscious patterns that limit our growth, authenticity, and fulfillment.

The healing and integration of the shadow empower sovereignty and our ability to navigate life with conscious awareness and intention.

The Path of Individuation

Shadow work is the gateway to individuation—the lifelong journey of becoming your most authentic and whole version of oneself. Individuation, a concept introduced by Carl Jung, refers to the process of self-awareness, integration, and alignment, where we learn to unite both our conscious and unconscious aspects.

Individuation and shadow work go hand in hand—true self-actualization requires integrating the shadow. Through this process, we break free from limiting beliefs, unconscious conditioning, and outdated self-perceptions, allowing us to step into deeper self-empowerment and wholeness.

Core Beliefs in Shadow Work Philosophy

Before we explore the practical stages of individuation, let's establish the fundamental principles that shape the philosophy of shadow work:

- **Self-Love as a Foundational Practice** — True transformation begins with deep self-love. Shadow work is an act of radical self-love—honoring all parts of yourself, even those that feel unworthy, broken, or hidden.
- **Awareness is Key** — Bringing the unconscious to light empowers self-mastery and intentional living.
- **Self-Acceptance is Power** — Embracing your shadow is essential for true healing and personal freedom.
- **Transformation through Integration** — Healing happens when we accept, learn from, and integrate our shadow rather than rejecting it.
- **Wholeness over Perfection** — The goal is integration, not "fixing" or erasing parts of yourself.

Ultimately, shadow work is a path to self-mastery. It allows us to heal old wounds, break free from negative cycles, and step into our authentic power. Through this process, we cultivate self-love, self-awareness, and personal liberation, aligning with our divine purpose and living more fully.

The Five Stages of the Path to Individuation

In our **Journey Within** e-course, we will explore what I have identified as the five stages of the Path to Individuation—an organic process that naturally fuels self-mastery. These stages are:

1. **Potential** — Recognizing the untapped energy within you.
2. **Identity & Capacity** — Understanding who you are and what you are capable of.
3. **Possibility** — Expanding your vision of "what's possible" beyond limitations.
4. **Adequacy** — Cultivating confidence in your ability to navigate changes and challenges.
5. **Personal Agency** — Embodying self-leadership and making empowered choices.

Each stage serves as a steppingstone, guiding you toward a deeper understanding of yourself and your authentic power.

E-COURSE LECTURE: "Becoming"

SECTION 4. PRINCIPLES

While the philosophy of shadow work provides the foundation, its principles serve as a practical guide for navigating the journey of self-exploration, healing, and integration. Philosophy answers the **"why,"** while principles outline the **"how."**

Shadow work is a journey of self-exploration, healing, and transformation. These principles outline the core steps of the process and how to engage in it effectively:

1. **Acknowledgment** — Recognizing the Shadow

The first step in shadow work is recognizing that everyone has a shadow self—the parts of us that have been suppressed due to societal conditioning, personal trauma, or fear. This includes unconscious patterns, hidden desires, wounds, and repressed emotions. Without acknowledgment, healing and integration cannot begin.

2. **Exploration** — Engaging in Deep Self-Inquiry

Once the shadow is recognized, the next step is to explore its depths. This requires introspection and self-examination, which can be done through meditation, journaling, therapy, dream analysis, or self-reflection exercises. The goal is to uncover the root causes behind our thoughts, behaviors, and emotional reactions.

3. Acceptance — Embracing Without Shame

Healing through shadow work requires radical acceptance—understanding that our shadow is not a flaw but a part of our human experience. What we resist, persists; suppressing the shadow only strengthens its unconscious hold on us. True healing comes from embracing these aspects without guilt, fear, or shame.

4. Integration — Owning and Transforming the Shadow

Integration is the process of making the unconscious conscious and actively working with our shadow rather than avoiding it. Instead of being controlled by hidden fears, wounds, or suppressed desires, we bring them into awareness, learn from them, and transform them into sources of wisdom and strength. But let's be clear—integration doesn't happen by simply acknowledging the shadow. It requires conscious action:

- Noticing triggers in real time
- Practicing new responses
- Making choices aligned with your higher self rather than old patterns

5. Transformation — Rewriting Old Patterns

Shadow work facilitates deep transformation by resolving inner conflicts, releasing emotional wounds, and breaking free from negative cycles. By confronting past experiences, unmet needs, and hidden fears, we rewrite old narratives and reclaim our full potential.

6. Self-Compassion — Navigating the Journey with Grace

Shadow work is not an easy process—it requires facing deep emotions, unresolved wounds, and uncomfortable truths. That's why self-compassion is essential. Being gentle with yourself, practicing patience, and approaching your healing with kindness makes the process more sustainable and empowering.

Shadow work isn't about 'finishing' your healing—it's an ongoing, spiral journey. You may revisit old wounds from new perspectives, and that's a sign of growth, not failure.

We'll dive deeply into these principles, exploring them in detail throughout the pages of this book. Shadow work is both a philosophy and a practice—a commitment to deep self-awareness, self-acceptance, and personal growth.

By embracing these principles, you empower yourself to heal, transform, and step into your most authentic self. This journey is one of radical self-love, profound healing, and ultimate freedom—and within these pages, you'll find the guidance and tools to fully embody it.

SECTION 5. PURPOSE AND BENEFITS

The purpose of shadow work is multifaceted and deeply transformative. Shadow work is a profound journey within, inviting us to embrace our inner work as an ongoing process of self-discovery and growth. It requires courage, patience, and self-compassion to delve into the depths of our psyche and confront the aspects of ourselves we may rather avoid.

Yet, through this courageous exploration, we uncover our true essence, unleash our most authentic selves, and reclaim our wholeness and divine purpose. By accepting both our light and shadow, we allow the full spectrum of our human experience to shine, learning to love and accept ourselves unconditionally within the grand tapestry of creation.

Shadow work invites us to unravel the mysteries of our unconscious, rediscovering our inherent beauty and wholeness. It is a path of transformation and liberation, leading to profound self-awareness, authenticity, and inner peace. As we embark on this journey, let us remember that within the darkness lies the seed of light and our divinity, waiting to be illuminated by the power of our own awareness.

Shadow work is often associated with healing deep trauma and wounds, but it offers a vast array of other transformative benefits that extend far beyond individual healing. By embracing the shadow and integrating its wisdom, we unlock greater resilience, personal transformation, and a deeper connection to our authentic selves.

Benefits of Shadow Work

- **Self-Awareness and Clarity** — Exploring your shadow provides profound insights into your values, desires, triggers, and motivations, fostering a clearer sense of self.

- **Healing and Emotional Release** — Provides tools to heal past wounds, releasing unresolved emotions and trauma, creating space for emotional growth.

- **Reparenting and Healing the Inner Child** — Provides space to heal childhood wounds and nurture yourself with love and compassion, building a healthier inner foundation.

- **Self-Worth and Vulnerability** — Shadow work teaches self-acceptance, embracing your flaws, and cultivating true self-worth while allowing vulnerability.

- **Emotional Intelligence and Resilience** — Shadow work strengthens emotional resilience by helping you face, process, and integrate difficult emotions with wisdom and ease.

- **Courage and Strength** — Confronting fears and insecurities builds inner strength, resilience, and the courage to face life's challenges.

- **Self-Empowerment** — Encourages reclaiming your personal power, increasing confidence and allowing you to stand strong in your authentic self.

JOURNEY WITHIN: DYNAMICS OF SHADOW WORK

- **Reframing Your Story** — Shadow work empowers you to rewrite limiting narratives and step into a future of personal growth and authenticity.
- **Healthy Relationships** — Integrating the shadow improves relationships by fostering authenticity, compassion, and emotional maturity, leading to deeper, aligned connections.
- **Creativity and Innovation** — Releases creative blocks, promoting the emergence of new ideas and fostering greater innovation.
- **Manifestation and Abundance** — Removes internal blocks to allow the flow of abundance in love, wealth, opportunities, and joy.
- **Personal Growth and Transformation** — Facilitates profound personal development, transcending limiting beliefs, and unlocking your highest potential.
- **Intuition and Spiritual Awareness** — Shadow work opens channels to your deeper wisdom, enhancing spiritual clarity and guiding you toward greater alignment.
- **Spiritual Awakening** — Shadow work is a gateway to deeper spiritual awakening. As you dissolve limiting beliefs, transmute past pain, and reclaim your authentic self, you align more fully with your soul's highest calling.
- **Alignment with Divine Purpose** — Shadow work helps shed limiting beliefs, aligning you with your true purpose for a more meaningful and fulfilling life.

Additional Benefits

- **Unlearning Conditioning** — Releases societal programming, creating space for authentic self-discovery.
- **Identifying and Overcoming Blocks to Self-Love** — Helps uncover internal barriers to self-acceptance.
- **Coping with Difficult Emotions** — Develops emotional resilience by addressing deep-seated feelings.
- **Releasing Codependency** — Encourages self-sufficiency and standing in your true power.
- **Establishing Boundaries** — Strengthens self-respect by teaching how to set and honor healthy limits.
- **Confidence in Life** — With greater self-awareness and empowerment, you navigate life with ease.
- **Jumping Timelines** — Transcends old versions of yourself, allowing you to step into your highest potential.

Ultimately, shadow work is a path to wholeness and liberation, empowering us to live more authentically and fully engage with life's richness and complexity.

SECTION 6. COMMON MISCONCEPTIONS

Despite its profound benefits, shadow work is often met with resistance and misconceptions. Some may fear delving into the depths of their psyche, fearing what they may uncover. Others may dismiss shadow work as indulging in negativity or dwelling on the past. However, it is important to recognize that shadow work is not about wallowing in darkness but rather about bringing light to the shadows to facilitate healing and transformation.

Misconceptions About Shadow Work

- **It's only about confronting darkness** — One common misconception is that shadow work is solely focused on confronting negative or dark aspects of the self. While it does involve exploring and integrating these aspects, shadow work also encompasses acknowledging and integrating positive but repressed traits, such as creativity, passion, and assertiveness. It's about embracing the full spectrum of our being, both light and shadow.

- **It's all about integrating the shadow** — One of the biggest mistakes in shadow work is trying to predict or control the outcome. Not all shadow work resolves with integration, sometimes it's about discernment, understanding, healing and eradication.

- **It's a quick fix or instant transformation** — Shadow work is often portrayed as a profound and transformative process, which it can be. However, it's essential to recognize that shadow work is a journey rather than a destination. It requires ongoing commitment, patience, and self-reflection. Real change takes time, and the process of integrating shadow aspects is not always linear. It's important to approach shadow work with realistic expectations and a willingness to engage in long-term inner exploration.

- **It's a one and done deal** — Shadow work is not a one-time experience. It needs patience, commitment and continuity as issues will reveal themselves one by one. Usually, the most urgent matters show up, but at times, issues we were not even aware of will show up for us to put all the pieces of the puzzle together.

- **Shadow work will make everything OK** — Shadow work won't eliminate pain or discomfort—it will reveal the root of your suffering, allowing you to release resistance, self-limiting beliefs, and unconscious self-sabotage. It will reveal why you are suffering, so you can get out of your own way, let go of the inner resistance, the self-limiting beliefs, and the self-sabotage causing you to feel pain and fear as you experience your upgrade.

- **It's only for those with deep trauma or psychological issues** — While shadow work can be particularly beneficial for individuals dealing with trauma or deep-seated psychological issues, it is not exclusive to those with extreme circumstances. Everyone has a shadow – aspects of the self that have been repressed or denied – regardless of their background or level of psychological health. Engaging in shadow work can benefit anyone seeking greater self-awareness, personal growth, and emotional healing.

- **It's dangerous or harmful** — Some people may fear that delving into the shadow will unearth overwhelming emotions or unleash negative energies that could be harmful. While it's true that shadow work can bring up uncomfortable feelings and challenging experiences, it is ultimately a process of healing and integration. When approached with mindfulness, self-compassion, and support, shadow work can be a safe and transformative journey. It's essential to proceed at a pace that feels comfortable and to seek guidance from trained professionals if needed.

- **It requires perfection or elimination of the shadow** — Another misconception is that shadow work aims to eliminate or eradicate the shadow entirely, leading to a state of perfection or enlightenment. In reality, the goal of shadow work is not to eliminate the shadow but to integrate it consciously into our sense of self. The shadow will always exist as a natural aspect of the human psyche, and our task is to develop a healthy relationship with it. Instead of striving for perfection, we aim for self-acceptance, compassion, and wholeness.

- **It's a solitary journey** — While shadow work often involves introspection and self-reflection, your practice can be amplified in collective spaces, such as healing circles, mentorship programs, or sacred partnerships where shared wisdom fosters deeper transformation. Seeking support from trusted friends, family members, or a therapist can provide valuable insights, perspective, and encouragement along the journey. Additionally, participating in group shadow work workshops or therapy sessions can offer a sense of community and shared experience, fostering deeper connections and understanding.

- **It's all about the inner child** — Although a great percentage of our issues generated during childhood or early development, we must not dismiss the possibility of facing issues with ancestral, generational, past life and karmic roots.

- **It's strictly psychological or emotional** — While shadow work primarily addresses psychological and emotional aspects of the self, it also has spiritual dimensions. Many spiritual traditions recognize the importance of shadow work in the process of self-realization and awakening. Engaging in practices such as meditation, contemplation, and ritual can deepen the spiritual aspects of shadow work, leading to profound insights and transformations.

- **It's just about self-improvement** — While shadow work can certainly lead to personal growth its ripple effects extend beyond the individual. By integrating our shadows, we break generational cycles, contribute to collective healing, and elevate human consciousness. True transformation radiates outward, shifting not just our personal reality but the world itself. We become more compassionate, empathetic, and understanding toward others as we learn to recognize and honor the interconnectedness of all beings and the importance of collective healing and transformation.

By addressing these misconceptions, individuals can approach shadow work with a clearer understanding of its nature, purpose, and potential benefits. Embracing the shadow is not only a journey of personal growth and transformation but also a path toward greater authenticity, wholeness, and connection with oneself and the world around us.

Know Thyself: Introspections 009-014

9. What is your present understanding or notion of shadow work?

10. Which shadow work benefit entirely resonates with you and your goals?

11. What motivates you to do the inner work?

12. What are you hoping the Journey Within framework helps you with?

13. Considering our entire portfolio of training, tools and resources, what additional support would you like to receive from us?

14. Did section 6 help you clarify any of your doubts, concerns or reservations about shadow work?

PHASE I

Contemplation and The Need to Shift

Journey Within Doorway #1. The Bench (The Call)

Once upon a time, amidst chaos, a familiar darkness echoed from within, louder than ever before, as if a fault line were forming in my heart. For as long as I can remember, I had sought to understand my depths, but this time, a nagging voice intruded on the "comfortable" life—or lie—I had created. Unwilling to face a "lightning strike" of reckoning, I ignored it, dismissing both my intuition and my shadows, convincing myself I could outsmart the inevitable by keeping it hidden.

For nearly three decades, I justified my self-imposed limitations with thoughts like, "Crying is for the weak," and I learned to live with an immeasurable weight of suppressed emotions.

I was destined for shadow work! In this incarnation, I came to Earth as a gifted rainbow child, born to an emotionally unavailable, submissive, and almost invisible mother, and a short-tempered, hyper-masculine "Don Juan" father. Together, they created a toxic dynamic of disempowerment and emotional neglect, wrapped in the rigid and judgmental environment where spiritual exploration outside their creed was neither encouraged nor safe.

Different, progressive, or unconventional ideas or behaviors were neither tolerated nor allowed. Yet here

I was—different, craving independence, and spiritually attuned—eager to experience life on my own terms. Deep within, I carried a knowing, like a sacred, encrypted code, that there was more to life than what I was enduring.

For the first 16 years of my life, I was confined, overprotected, discouraged, and constantly judged. I was taught conditional love, which fed my self-loathing. My uniqueness became a source of shame and guilt that I internalized deeply. My spiritual gifts were suppressed, my sexuality denied, and I convinced myself I didn't deserve love.

And yet, beneath the weight of it all, I knew I was meant to break a generational curse rooted in self-hatred and denial. It was my sacred mission to become my authentic self. But how could I—this disempowered version of myself—undertake such a daunting task? Where would I find the key to unlock my shackles? I didn't feel capable or worthy of such a royal task.

Still, no self-doubt or self-loathing could deter my soul's divine calling. My akasha was a solid code, incorruptible and truly unf*ckable-with. Love—the universal love of the Creator—broke through every defense. When love takes over, resistance crumbles, and transformation begins.

At 19, my emancipation marked the start of a new chapter—a life where I could "be free" and make my own decisions. But taking off the shackles is one thing; truly understanding a life without restraints is another.

For the next decade I threw myself into work and the monotony of daily life, using busyness as a distraction. I explored relationships without ever questioning what love truly meant, unaware that I had never witnessed or experienced a healthy one. Though the physical cage was gone, I remained trapped in an invisible prison, unable to understand or receive love. Most of all, I didn't know how to love myself.

I spent my entire childhood suppressing my spiritual gifts, my teenage years denying my sexuality, and much of my adulthood pretending I was content without experiencing real, heart-to-heart love. As a coping mechanism, I had already built a wall around my heart, suppressing emotional engagement and developing a control-freak personality to ensure my safety. Unconsciously, I had internalized self-hatred as a core part of my identity and accepted shallow, pretend connections as all I deserved.

The "lightning strike" of reckoning that eventually brought me to my knees was a harsh and unapologetic rude awakening. At the time, I was consumed with building my business and enduring a loveless marriage. I had mastered the art of pretending—pretending I was okay, pretending I was happy, pretending I was normal, pretending I was straight, and most of all, pretending I was in control. That last one? The biggest delusion of them all.

I remember it like it was yesterday.

In 2009, on the morning of my first expo conference, I was in a hotel room getting ready for the event. I was excited to head downstairs for breakfast and greet my vendors. As I grabbed my bag and approached the door, a sudden, sharp pain stabbed my chest. It felt like an elephant was sitting on me. I genuinely thought I was having a heart attack.

My ex-husband and son were in the room, but their images began fading, as if they were slipping away. I felt completely alone, spiraling into a downward vortex, like standing in the eye of a tornado.

I had no choice but to collapse onto the floor, gasping for air as my most hateful inner critic took over, screaming:

"Where do you think you're going?"

"Who do you think you are?"

"You're not good enough."

A whisper, almost drowned out: "That's not true."

"Everyone will know how gay and empty you are."

"How pathetic!"

"They can see through your bullshit, you f*cking weirdo."

Yet, I felt the quiet evidence of something real "You are more."

I was trapped in the throes of an unexpected panic attack, fueled by years of self-hatred, and it lasted nearly two hours. Looking back now, with the understanding I've gained, I realize I was utterly crippled by fear. The only way I could have regained my breath and calmed down was by allowing myself to feel my emotions and cry. But that wasn't an option then. Crying? Absolutely not. "What kind of boss-bitch cries? That's lame." My ego intercepted.

"Crying is for the weak," it scolded, echoing the voice of my now-deceased father: "Why are you crying? I'll give you a reason to cry."

That moment was my rude awakening. It was meant to be a precious "Tower" moment—a divine intervention offering me the chance to rebuild my foundation. But I chose to ignore it, pretending it never happened. Somehow, I managed to stand up, leave that room, and walk straight into the ballroom to host my event. "I guess I was just a little stressed about the show," I told myself. "I'm fine." But I wasn't fine.

Yes, I chose to ignore the call, and the Universe wasn't finished with me.

That moment was only the beginning.

Sooner rather than later, I would be summoned to *The Bench* again.

ILLUMINATION
I'll Let You Borrow My Lantern

I am here, holding the light for you. For now, I carry this lantern so you can see the path ahead—until the moment you no longer need my flame, because you have found your own.

For most of my life, I felt like I was speaking a language no one else could understand. My thoughts moved too fast, my emotions ran too deep, and my truth was too abstract for others to follow. Conversations often felt like puzzles—my words never quite fitting the way I intended. It was as if I carried a vast, intricate world inside me, but no clear way to translate it into something others could grasp.

It wasn't until later in life that I was formally diagnosed as on the autistic spectrum. That revelation brought clarity—it explained why emotions had always been so difficult to navigate. Why channeling, expressing, and even recognizing them sometimes felt like an uphill battle. Beyond that, I struggled to communicate my insights in ways that others could understand or keep up with. My inner world was rich, nuanced, and layered—but it often felt like an encrypted language that few could decipher.

For years, I searched for a bridge—a way to bring my internal landscape into the external world without losing its depth or truth. That's when I found Tarot. It wasn't just a tool; it was a **lifeline**. A **language**. A **mirror**. Tarot gave structure to the insights that had always existed within me but had felt just out of reach. It became my means of articulation, turning intuition into something tangible, emotions into symbols, and the unseen into something I could finally **see**.

More than just a spiritual practice, Tarot became my **greatest ally in self-mastery and creative self-expression**. It helped me decode and share the wisdom buried deep within my psyche, transforming my intuitive knowing into something that could be understood and felt—not just by me, but by others. The cards reflected my unspoken truths, revealed my hidden shadows, and became both a guide and a companion on my journey of self-discovery.

Through Tarot, I learned to embrace my intuitive gifts and find meaningful ways to connect with the world. It became both **a language and a liberation**—a way to honor my neurodivergent experience while expressing my truth with clarity and confidence. Tarot is not just an extension of my inner world; it is the **key** that unlocks it, turning the abstract into something that can be seen, felt, and understood.

To stay true to myself and honor you with my most authentic energy, I will integrate **Tarot narratives and illuminations** as part of the storytelling in this book. But don't worry—whether you're fluent in Tarot's language or have never touched a deck before, you'll still find meaning woven throughout these pages.

Tarot, in my perspective, is the **storytelling of life**, and our **Journey Within** is beautifully encapsulated in what we call **The Fool's Journey**. This journey represents the milestones of personal transformation, as symbolized by the

Major Arcana. Each card reflects a crucial step in self-discovery, growth, and mastery.

In my **Tarot for Self-Mastery Masterclass**, I present this narrative through the lens of **shadow work**, focusing on how The Fool evolves into **The Fool 2.0**—a version of themselves refined by deep inner work, radical self-awareness, and profound self-realization.

Joseph Campbell, a renowned author and teacher influenced by Carl Jung's philosophy, is best known for his work on **The Hero's Journey**—a universal narrative of transformation found in myths, legends, and storytelling. While Campbell never directly linked his framework to Tarot, modern scholars and spiritual practitioners have drawn clear parallels between his work and the archetypal wisdom of the Major Arcana. Both explore universal patterns of growth, challenge, and transcendence.

However, there is a key difference:

- **The Hero's Journey** is an **outward** quest—facing external trials, slaying dragons, and proving one's worth through action.
- **The Fool's Journey** is an **inward** quest—confronting inner demons, breaking through limiting beliefs, and uncovering one's own truth.

Where the Hero wields a sword to defeat their foes, the Fool wields self-awareness—the sharpest weapon of all.

The Fool's Journey vs. The Hero's Journey

Yet, both journeys are reflections of one another. Every Hero must transform internally to conquer their external trials, and every Fool must embrace their inner heroism to transcend their own limitations. The Fool's Journey is the embodiment of the shadow work process, where self-mastery is forged through trial, introspection, and integration.

Through this lens, The Fool evolves into the Hero, and ultimately, The Fool 2.0—the version of themselves who has embraced self-discovery, navigated both internal and external challenges, and emerged more self-aware, resilient, and whole.

The Journey Within: A Roadmap to Self-Mastery

We're going to use this classic metaphor to illustrate the dynamics and power of shadow work—the deep, transformational process that unfolds as we journey within. This synthesis of external and internal milestones mirrors the universal process of self-realization, expressed through these key phases:

1. **Unrealized Potential** — The dormant self, unaware of what lies ahead.
2. **The Call to Adventure** — The spark that ignites the journey.
3. **Acceptance (or Refusal) of the Call** — The moment of resistance or surrender.

CONCEPTS

4. **Meeting the Mentors** — Guidance from within or from wise teachers.
5. **Crossing the Threshold** — The leap into transformation.
6. **Facing Tests, Allies, and Enemies** — Confronting internal and external forces.
7. **Accessing the Innermost** — A deep descent into the self.
8. **Experiencing the Ordeal** — The dark night of the soul, where shadows are faced.
9. **Receiving the Reward** — The wisdom and integration gained from struggle.
10. **Returning Transformed** — Rebirth into a higher self.
11. **Sharing the Gift** — Spreading the lessons learned, embodying self-mastery.

Some journeys begin in shadows. Not because they are meant to stay there, but because the eyes must first adjust to truly see. So I will walk with you for a time, lantern in hand, until your own fire burns bright enough to light the way.

Eventually, every seeker must find their own lantern. Some find it in their intuition. Some in their experiences. And some in the cards—pages of a story waiting to be read.

I created *The Lantern Tarot Oracle* for those who seek depth and clarity through Tarot—for heart-centered souls who wish to ignite and cultivate their own light. My deck was born from the same fire that has shaped and guided me, crafted to be a beacon—illuminating what has always been there, waiting to be seen.

JOURNEY WITHIN: DYNAMICS OF SHADOW WORK

As we move forward, I will weave Tarot archetypes and rich storytelling into our exploration, using the Hero's milestones both as a map and a mirror for our soul's unfolding journey.

So, are you ready to embark on your own Fool's Journey? To become the Hero and protagonist of your story? To face your shadows, embrace your wisdom, and step fully into your own mastery?

If so, let's begin.

Onward.

HERO'S MILESTONE 1
Unrealized Potential

Have you ever felt that tugging sense that there's something more to life?

Have you ever experienced moments that made you feel like you were standing on the edge of something vast and unknown?

In life, there comes a moment when we're called to step into something new—whether it's a new job, a new relationship, a new way of thinking, or an unexpected challenge that pushes us outside our comfort zone. This "call" can show up in many forms: a sudden realization, an alluring opportunity, a new burning desire, or simply a feeling that things can't stay the same anymore.

The Call to Adventure is the moment when life nudges us, often through a sense of dissatisfaction or longing, toward something greater. It's a reminder that there's more to our life story than what we've known so far. The call is a signal that it's time to move forward into a new chapter. This moment can feel exciting, scary, or both—like a whisper encouraging us to take a leap of faith into the unknown.

Before the call is made and before the adventure truly begins, there exists the boundless potential represented by **The Fool**. This phase represents the moment before the journey takes shape—the essence of limitless possibilities.

The **Fool** stands at the edge of the unknown, with wide-eyed curiosity. With no expectations or preconceived notions, they embrace the journey ahead. This space is open to growth, transformation, and self-discovery. It marks the birth of new possibilities and the raw, unshaped potential within each of us. The Fool's Journey is an invitation to step into the unknown, without knowing the full scope of the challenges or rewards, but ready to explore and evolve.

This phase, the 'Unrealized Potential' milestone, represents a state of being where the Fool is unaware of their latent abilities, strengths, or purpose. The universe knows the hero's potential and has already laid the groundwork for their journey, but the Fool remains in a state of innocence, naiveté, or unknowing. They may feel disconnected or lost, sensing that something is missing, but not knowing exactly what it is.

During this time, the Fool holds the seeds of greatness within them, but these seeds have yet to sprout. They don't see themselves as a hero and may not yet feel ready to step into the role meant for them. This phase can be perplexing, as there is an inner knowing of a greater purpose, yet no clarity on its form.

I can deeply relate to this state. Even though I was always "spiritually inclined," and despite the conditioning I was exposed to, I always knew there was something more I was meant to do with my life. However, I had no idea of the magnitude of my mission or the complexity of my divine plan. Feeling lost was an understatement. It wasn't just a feeling—it was a knowing, an understanding that I wasn't of this world, but for this world.

There's a deep, inexplicable feeling within us that we don't always understand, but it's always been there. It's like a whisper in the background of our consciousness. You might have moments when you feel like you don't belong here, you're not on the right path, or that you're connected to something greater than yourself. It's as if your soul knows you're here for a special reason, but you can't quite figure out what that reason is.

In these moments, the mundane aspects of daily life—the routine hustle and familiarity—become insignificant and meaningless. It's as though you're standing at the edge of something vast, caught between the world you know and the pull of something much bigger, something cosmic.

You might feel drawn to the stars, to the mysteries of the universe, as though you've always been attuned to them. There is thirst for knowledge. There's a longing for truth that goes beyond earthly concerns—a longing for something higher, something more. This feeling is both magical and unsettling—a recognition of something vast and untapped within.

This unknown potential is a calling that we haven't fully understood. It's the whisper of a future version of ourselves—a version that has already walked this journey, accomplished great things, and aligned with our true self. This future self knows exactly what we are capable of, but right now, we're only scratching the surface.

Even without fully understanding what's happening inside us, there is soul-level recognition. Our soul is trying to remember who it truly is. When we align with this knowing, our lives begin to change. We start noticing synchronicities, feeling more attuned to our higher self, and attracting people, events, or teachings that confirm our true nature.

The important thing to remember is that this feeling—this deep yearning or sense of cosmic purpose—is valid, even without a label. If you've ever felt that pull, that sense of being connected to something greater, that's your soul nudging you toward its awakening. The universe knows your divine mission, and even if you don't fully understand it yet, you are already on the path to discovering it.

The Universe's Viewpoint

The Universe has already set things in motion. The path is waiting. The signs are appearing. The moment you decide to pay attention, the journey begins.

The divine energy already knows the Fool's power and greatness—it's all about divine timing and guiding them toward the realization of their purpose. This is where synchronicities, quiet nudges, and subtle signs begin to emerge, inviting the Fool to pay attention, without fully understanding why or how.

This stage mirrors the idea of hidden potential—the universe knows what lies beneath the surface, but the Fool has yet to recognize it in themselves. There's an invisible thread connecting the Fool to their true path, and the universe is preparing the way for them to step into their destiny.

Characteristics of Unrealized Potential:

- **Dormant Gifts:** The Fool has inherent talents, wisdom, and purpose that are not yet fully accessed. These are the gifts that will emerge later in the journey but remain hidden for now.

- **Yearning Without Knowing Why:** There's a sense that something is missing, a longing for purpose or fulfillment, but the Fool can't yet articulate it. They might feel restless, like there's something more, but they're unsure of what it is.

- **The Fear of the Unknown:** The Fool may feel hesitant or fearful of stepping into the unknown. While they sense there is something greater out there, they might resist or avoid change because of uncertainty about what's to come.

- **External Distractions:** The Fool might be deeply enmeshed in the practicalities of daily life, which creates a veil over their deeper purpose. They are living through the motions, unaware of the larger cosmic plan in play.

- **Limited Self-Perception:** At this stage, the Fool likely doesn't see themselves as a hero. They might doubt their worth or believe that their potential is too far out of reach, completely unaware of the powerful force that resides within them.

- **The Unseen Road:** The universe knows the path and is already nudging the Fool toward it, often through chance encounters, synchronistic events, or the feeling of "a calling" that seems to come out of nowhere. However, the Fool is still on the edge, unsure of the journey ahead.

And then, it happens. The moment of activation. A shift in energy, an undeniable invitation from the Universe. The Fool is no longer just standing at the edge—they are being called forward. Will they answer?

This is where the universe begins to make it clear: it's time to awaken, to recognize the greatness within, and to step into a higher purpose. The call may come as a sudden realization, an external event, or a deep inner knowing. The Fool, at this point, begins to see that their life has a greater meaning, and their journey toward self-actualization is about to begin.

HERO'S MILESTONE 2
The Call to Adventure

In the Fool's Journey, The Call to Adventure is the moment when innocence and unlimited potential meet the first challenge. The Fool stands on the precipice of leaving innocence behind and embarking on a transformational path. It's the pivotal moment when The Fool is invited—or pushed—into engaging with life in a way that challenges their comfort zone, beliefs, or naivety.

This invitation stirs excitement and fear, igniting an energetic shift that may lead to determination or hesitation. Often, a mentor figure such as The Magician or The High Priestess appears, offering wisdom, support, tools, or a glimpse of higher purpose to guide The Fool forward.

You can likely anticipate how our Journey Within sacred milestones align with the Hero's journey storyline but allow me to elaborate further to ensure clarity and keep you on the right path.

The Call to Adventure often feels like being "summoned to The Bench." This is a sacred moment of contemplation, where the traveler—whether it's you or me—sits with their current self, reflecting on life's struggles and recognizing the need for change. It's a reality check, a moment when the call whispers: "It's time to let go of the pain you carry and rise to your highest potential."

But here's the twist: we have free will. The Fool can accept the call—or refuse it.

ILLUMINATION

The Bench is not merely a physical object, but the contemplation and recognition of our soul's whispers. It feels timeless, solid beneath you, yet somehow, it cradles your being in a way that transcends the ordinary.

Its surface is weathered, the wood softened by years of touch, yet the grain remains strong—like the wisdom of generations whispered through its very fibers. It is not just a place to sit; it is a threshold, a quiet space that exists between worlds. The moment you approach, a subtle weight lingers in the air, as though the universe itself holds its breath.

As you sit, the wood molds to your form—not in comfort, but in a way that demands stillness. An invitation to surrender, to pause, to listen. You know the call has been made: **it is time to choose yourself.**

It hums with a faint vibration, something ancient and deep, as if it understands the weight of your questions and the stirring in your heart. The coolness of its surface contrasts with the warmth of your body, grounding you in the present while calling you forward into what is yet to come.

Beneath you, the earth is steady, holding you up, yet alive—rooted in the sacredness of this moment. The air is thick with possibility, carrying the scent of damp earth and growing things, as if the very space is pregnant with change. Each breath you take is filled with the promise of release and renewal.

CONCEPTS

The Bench offers no judgment or demands—only space. A stillness before the storm of transformation. A pause before the leap. It invites you to look inward, to reflect on the life you have lived, and gently urges you to let go. This is where the call is heard—not with fanfare or force, but in the soft whisper of your own soul, urging you to rise beyond pain and embrace the next step of your journey.

Being summoned to The Bench feels like the sudden stillness before a storm—an invisible force that halts you in your tracks. A deep, magnetic pull draws you closer, and as you approach, you sense a subtle weight in the air, as if the universe has paused to give you this moment. Your heart beats a little faster—not from fear, but from the quiet recognition that this is a threshold, a liminal space between who you are and who you are about to become.

As you sit, there is an instant sensation of both heaviness and release. The weight of your past—your struggles, your pains, the burdens you carry—settles into your bones, making your shoulders heavy and your breath a little shallow. Yet, at the same time, there is a strange lightness, as though The Bench itself is offering you permission to let go. The air pulses around you, thick with energy, aligning everything for this moment of reckoning.

In the quiet, the world feels distant. Time stretches and folds, yet it is as if you are stepping into eternity. Your thoughts race, yet in the pit of your stomach, there is an undeniable knowing—a truth rising from within. You are aware of your old patterns, your fears, your excuses. But something in the very fabric of this moment calls you to rise above them. You cannot remain the same. You are being asked to shed the old skin, to release what no longer serves you, to step into a higher version of yourself.

The Bench does not speak. Yet, it holds you in its steady embrace, offering no distraction, no comfort—only the space to hear the quiet call from deep within. It is the whisper of your soul, the quiet realization that change is no longer optional.

There comes a moment when the soul's whispers intensify to a level that can no longer be ignored. It is a calling—an awakening—to assess the imbalances, the suffering, the lack, and all that has been holding us back. The universe places us on a bench—a sacred pause—to contemplate and make a choice. It is here that we begin to feel the weight of what needs healing and the spark of what could be. On this bench, decisions are made: will we continue on as we are, or will we embrace the unknown journey toward transformation?

The Bench is a sacred and transformative pause—a divinely orchestrated moment urging us to stop, reflect, and connect deeply with our soul's truth. More than a physical seat, it represents a metaphysical space where we confront the whispers of our inner being, often brought into focus by challenges, suffering, imbalances, or unfulfilled desires.

The Bench is not a place of rest. It is a state of contemplation.

Whether we accept or reject the call, we will never be the same. The question has been asked, the awareness has settled in, and the knowing lingers—silent yet undeniable. There is no way back to before.

The Bench does not grant answers; it offers a mirror. And once seen, cannot be unseen. A whisper stirs at the edge of the soul, growing louder the longer we sit. There is no pressure, only presence. But something has shifted, and we know it.

We've all been there—that moment when we feel 'enough is enough' or 'I'm done with this.

That moment is a point of reckoning—the pause where we realize we can't continue as we have. The awareness has settled in. The knowing lingers.

The only question left is: Will we answer the call, or will we stay where we are?

The Bench doesn't force action. But it makes it impossible to ignore the truth. And the choice is no longer if we will answer—but when.

The Bench isn't just a moment of reflection—it's a reckoning.

For example:

- Someone struggles too hard for too long, and their body, mind or sprit finally shuts down. In the forced stillness, a truth emerges: *"I can't keep living like this."* The Bench asks: **Will we continue this cycle, or choose balance and well-being?**
- We stay in a relationship that drains us, convincing ourselves it's fine—until one day, we can't. *"I deserve more than this."* The Bench asks: **Will we keep settling, or will we choose ourselves?**
- A dream lingers in our heart, but we keep playing it safe. Then life shakes us awake: *"If I don't follow my purpose now, I never will."* The Bench asks: **Will we keep hiding, or will we finally step into our calling?**

Not everyone hears the call the first time. Some resist. Some deny it. Some pretend they never heard it at all.

Know Thyself: Introspections 015

15. The Bench: What areas of your life feel out of alignment, unauthentic or stagnant, and how are you contributing to this imbalance?

OUR JOURNEY

- **The Fool** — A fresh clean slate, unlimited potential.

- **The Magician** — You have the power and resources to solve your problems.

- **The Chariot** — Your inner quest, determination, and control over your direction.

CHAPTER TWO
DYNAMICS

SECTION 7. AWARENESS

Shadow work is the path of integration, a descent into the unseen self. **Awareness is the threshold into this journey**—the moment light is cast into the depths of the unconscious. Without awareness, the shadow remains hidden, ruling from beneath the surface.

Every journey inward begins with a moment of awareness—a moment where something no longer fits, where discomfort rises, where we can no longer ignore what has been lurking in the dark.

Awareness is the foundation of transformation and it deepens as we recognize, challenge and confront the conflict between who we think we are and who we truly are—the first crack in the illusion of unconscious living. It is the ability to observe thoughts, emotions, behaviors, and patterns without immediate attachment. Before self-awareness, before individuation, before radical self-love—there is simply awareness: the recognition that "something" is.

Awareness vs. Self-Awareness

Many assume that awareness and self-awareness are interchangeable, but they are not. Awareness is external and internal observation, while self-awareness is personal, introspective, and self-referential.

- Awareness is when you notice a repeating relationship pattern.
- Self-awareness is when you recognize your role in it.

Awareness sees the cycles; self-awareness questions their origins. Awareness acknowledges external influences; self-awareness dissects their impact on identity. Awareness begins the journey; self-awareness chooses to walk the path.

True self-awareness is confronting the conditioning that shaped you—your learned beliefs, inherited trauma, social programming—and choosing who you are beyond it.

The Pitfalls of Self-Awareness

Self-awareness is necessary, and crucial, but it is not the final destination. Many get trapped in the intellectualization of self-awareness, mistaking understanding for transformation.

- **Over-identification:** Becoming attached to labels (e.g., "I have abandonment wounds" or "I'm an empath") without doing the work to transcend them.
- **Analysis Paralysis:** Endless introspection without action, leading to stagnation.
- **Self-Judgment:** Using awareness as a tool for shame rather than empowerment.

The danger? The illusion that awareness is enough. Recognition without integration keeps a person stuck in cycles of knowing but not growing. The work is in bridging the gap between awareness and individuation—moving from seeing to becoming.

Let's circle back to shadow work's philosophy of becoming the most authentic, whole version of oneself through the process of individuation—the uniting of both our conscious and unconscious aspects.

Individuation is the **reclamation of true essence**—who you are beyond conditioning, wounds, and societal expectations.

The gap between **awareness and individuation** is **choice**:

- The choice to dismantle false identities.
- The choice to embody the wisdom awareness reveals.
- The choice to align with the self beyond programming.

This is shadow work. This is individuation. This is the path back to whole self.

A person can know they 'people-please' but still struggle to set boundaries. They can understand their fears but still live in avoidance. The bridge from awareness to individuation is action—through radical self-honesty, self-compassion, and courage.

Individuation demands the death of the conditioned self. It asks: Who are you beneath survival mechanisms? Beneath expectations? Beneath what the world told you to be?

This is where the sense of self and true essence emerge. The sense of self is shaped by roles, identity markers, and life experiences. True essence is what remains when all of that is stripped away. It is sovereign, unshaken, eternal.

True essence is the unconditioned self—the part of you that existed before you were named, shaped, or taught who to be. It is not found, but remembered. It is the whisper beneath survival instincts, the knowing before logic interferes.

Most people live their lives as reflections of expectation, with identities crafted in response to external forces. But individuation requires deconstructing and unlearning conditioning, so that what has always been -your true essence- can emerge.

In the Hero's Journey, self-awareness is the moment the protagonist recognizes they can no longer return to who they once were. It is the Call to Adventure—the disruption of unconscious existence—and the Refusal of the Call, when fear and resistance arise.

- **The Fool (0)** begins in unawareness.
- **The Magician (I)** realizes power.
- **The High Priestess (II)** observes truth.
- **The Chariot (VII)** decides to move.

True self-awareness is not just seeing oneself as a character in their story, but as the author or co-creator. Yes, the Call to Adventure is the disruption of unconscious existence.

But what happens next?

- **The Chariot (VII)** is the moment of decision—the drive to move forward, even when fear lingers. It is the conscious effort to take control of the journey rather than letting fate dictate the path.

So, where are you right now?

Are you still gathering awareness, like The Fool—sensing that something is shifting?

Are you taking the reins, like The Chariot—ready to move with purpose?

Or are you ready to take the leap, eager to embody your true essence?

Maybe you've been stuck in cycles of self-reflection, feeling the weight of what you know but unsure how to bridge the gap. If so, you are not alone. The space between awareness and individuation can feel vast, but it is not impassable.

To close this gap, one must move beyond awareness, strip away illusions of self and align with true essence. The journey is not just to know oneself—but to embody the true self beyond conditioning.

SECTION 8. REALIZATION

Realization is the moment of profound understanding—an internal shift where something previously unseen, misunderstood, or unacknowledged becomes undeniably clear.

It is the "aha" moment when awareness moves beyond observation into deep knowing. Unlike awareness, which is the recognition of something's existence, realization is the embodiment of truth—it changes perception, emotions, and often, actions.

In shadow work, realization is the catalyst for transformation. It is when a person not only sees their patterns but feels the truth of them in a way that makes change inevitable. It is the moment a survival mechanism is exposed, a limiting belief is dismantled, or an illusion shatters—paving the way for conscious evolution.

Awareness is about noticing something, becoming conscious of our thoughts, emotions, behaviors, or patterns. But it is neutral; we observe without necessarily understanding or acting on it yet. Realization is the deeper comprehension of what awareness has revealed.

For example (Awareness) "I keep self-sabotaging my success." vs. (Realization) "I self-sabotage because deep down, I fear failure and rejection due to past wounds."

Awareness vs. Realization vs. Self-Realization

Awareness is when you notice something. It's the first crack in the illusion.

"I see my pattern. I recognize my triggers."

Realization is when that awareness lands—when it clicks in a way that you can't ignore. It's not just knowing; it's feeling the truth hit you.

"Oh. This is why I do this. This is where it comes from."

Self-Realization is when that truth rewires you. It's no longer a thought—it's a shift in your being.

"This no longer controls me. I am choosing differently."

Realization as a Catalyst, Awareness as a Threshold

- Awareness opens the door. You stand there, looking at what's inside, but you haven't stepped through yet.

- Realization is what pushes you through. It's that undeniable moment when something changes inside of you. Once you realize, you can't un-realize.

Example: Imagine you've always felt unseen by romantic partners. And then "out of the blue" after your last breakup in a split second something clicks!—not just mentally, but in your body and soul. It's the truth landing so hard that you can't ignore it anymore.

- Awareness is noticing the pattern. "I always attract emotionally unavailable people."

- Realization is the "aha!" moment. "Omg ... I've been chasing the love I never got as a child."

- Self-Realization is when it fully integrates. "I don't need to chase anymore. I can give myself the love I seek."

How Realization May Feel in the Body

Realization isn't just a thought. It hits differently—it's a shift in your being!

- **Physically:** A deep exhale. A tightness release. A weight lifted off your chest. A gut drop like the floor just disappeared from under you.
- **Energetically:** A rush. A wave of clarity. A sense of calm. A deep stillness inside.
- **Emotionally:** A mix of grief and freedom. A mourning of who you were. A relief in knowing you're not that anymore.

Awareness opens the door. Realization walks you through it. Self-realization locks it behind you—because there's no going back.

E-COURSE LECTURE: "From Self-Discovery to Self-Mastery"

SECTION 9. FORCES AT WORK

In my shadow work practice—whether working one-on-one with clients or leading our weekly One Vessel Devotion sessions—I explore shadow narratives and recurring themes through three key aspects: energy, mindset, and emotions.

These aspects reveal our predominant vibrational state—the energetic signature we unconsciously operate from. By understanding them, we gain insight into our hidden patterns, blockages, and the pathways to transformation.

- **Energy** reflects how we hold and move through life. It shows where our power is blocked, where it leaks, and where it needs to be reclaimed.
- **Mindset** reveals the belief systems shaping our reality. It determines whether we operate from expansion or limitation, whether we navigate life as creators or as victims of circumstance.
- **Emotions** serve as both messengers and gateways. What we suppress controls us. What we integrate empowers us.

By working with shadow profiles through these three aspects, we gain a clearer picture of where we are energetically, mentally, and emotionally—and more importantly, how to shift into alignment with our true essence.

Energy: The Frequency You Operate From

At our core, we are **energy**. Every thought, emotion, and action carries a frequency that either aligns with expansion or contraction, love or fear, liberation or limitation. Shadow work is the process of recognizing, understanding, and ultimately transforming the energy we hold within.

- **Understanding Energy** — Shadow work is about recognizing and working with different frequencies within ourselves, including both light and shadow aspects.

- **Transmutation vs. Amplification: Energy is neither good nor bad** — it is either transmuted or amplified. If left unchecked, lower vibrational energies (such as fear, guilt, and shame) will continue to reinforce unconscious patterns. But when acknowledged and worked through, these same energies can be alchemized into wisdom, empowerment, and love.

- **Energetic Awareness: What we suppress doesn't disappear** — it buries itself deep in our energetic field, influencing our reality from the shadows. Becoming aware of our energetic patterns allows us to break cycles, shift frequencies, and reclaim our power.

- **Balance and Integration** — True energetic mastery comes from integrating both light and shadow aspects. The goal isn't to eliminate shadow but to acknowledge, integrate, and harmonize it. This creates an inner equilibrium, fostering a sense of wholeness and alignment.

JOURNEY WITHIN: DYNAMICS OF SHADOW WORK

Your energy is your vibrational signature—it speaks before you do, attracts what you believe you deserve, and determines the quality of your reality. If you want a different life, you must shift your frequency.

When we shift our energy, our mindset follows. The beliefs we hold shape the frequency we emit, influencing how we experience reality.

Mindset: The Architect of Your Reality

When working with our mindset profile, we examine the old paradigms and self-limiting beliefs that shape our reality. This includes negativity, codependencies, attachments to scarcity, and a deep-seated sense of unworthiness—all of which keep us stagnant and disconnected from our true potential.

Mindset dictates everything—who we are, what we believe is possible, and what we allow ourselves to experience. It's the silent architect of our reality. It governs both our conscious and subconscious cores shaping our beliefs, perceptions, and experiences. It influences:

- How we view reality (paradigm processes).
- How we think and create (cognitive functions).
- How we feel, act, attract and relate to others (human experience).

If we want true transformation, we must prioritize **self-awareness, mindfulness, and conscious paradigm-shifting**. This means actively reshaping our mindset to focus on what we want to achieve, rather than reinforcing self-defeating patterns and the illusion of limitations.

Everything you are, everything you do, and every connection you form is influenced by your mindset. It's not just important—it's the foundation of your life.

- **Awareness** — Shadow work starts with self-awareness—recognizing patterns, beliefs, and behaviors that stem from the unconscious.
- **Reframing** — It challenges us to shift perspectives, seeing struggles as gateways to growth rather than obstacles. This involves identifying and dismantling limiting beliefs.
- **Mindfulness** — Developing mindfulness allows us to observe thoughts and emotions without immediate reaction, creating space for conscious choice and transformation.

Our emotions reinforce our mindset. If our mind is programmed by fear or scarcity, our emotions will reflect and perpetuate that cycle.

Emotions: The Unprocessed Stories We Carry

Emotions are energy in motion—the way our body communicates unresolved experiences, unmet needs, and buried truths. Shadow work demands that we face these emotions without judgment so they can be fully processed, integrated, and transformed.

JOURNEY WITHIN: DYNAMICS OF SHADOW WORK

- **Exploring the Emotional Body** — Shadow work brings suppressed or repressed emotions to the surface, allowing them to be acknowledged and understood. Many of our emotional patterns are imprints from childhood, past experiences, and generational wounds. Until we become conscious of them, we will continue to repeat the same loops—mistaking them for fate when they are really unprocessed emotions seeking acknowledgment.

- **Healing the Wounds** — It requires addressing past pain, trauma, and unresolved conflicts that shape our shadow selves. Avoidance doesn't make emotions disappear; it makes them louder in different ways—manifesting as anxiety, resentment, burnout, or even physical ailments. Healing requires facing the emotions, sitting with them, and allowing them to teach us what we need to integrate.

- **Emotional Alchemy** — Self-compassion is the key to emotional healing. Instead of rejecting our wounds, we must learn to witness them with love. Through this process, our greatest pains become our greatest teachers. True transformation comes through radical self-acceptance, embracing even the parts of ourselves we once rejected. Your emotions are not your enemy—they are your guide. They show you where healing is needed and where liberation is possible.

By working through energy, mindset, and emotions, we reclaim our power. We stop living on autopilot and start creating with intention. Shadow work is not about erasing our wounds—it is about integrating them into our strength. The path to wholeness is not through avoidance but through radical self-acceptance.

Know Thyself: Introspections 016-021

16. **Awareness:** Where do I feel the greatest disconnect between my inner truth and how I show up in the world?

17. **Realization:** What recurring emotions, thoughts, or behaviors reveal who I have been conditioned to be versus who I truly am?

18. **Self-Realization:** What inner truth am I ready to reclaim and embody as I step into deeper self-ownership?

19. **Energy:** Where am I leaking or misdirecting my energy, and how can I reclaim it to align with my highest self?

20. **Mindset:** What recurring negative beliefs or thought patterns keep me stuck, and how can I begin to shift them toward a more empowering perspective?

21. **Emotion:** What unprocessed or suppressed emotions are influencing my reactions, and how can I create space to feel and heal them?

SECTION 10. SOUL WHISPERS

Based on my many solar returns—and the way I experience and witness the impact of my energy—I consider myself a catalyst of change.

Whether you encounter my presence personally or professionally, and whether I remain for a paragraph, a page, or a chapter in your book of life...

Transformation follows. And trust me here, I am <u>not</u> bragging.

And as you read this, I am anchoring and radiating this intention for you, wherever you are. I am here, advocating for your transformation and inviting you to embrace your shadow work journey wholeheartedly—because you deserve to experience your most authentic vibration and the best life possible.

This is a message from the Universe, a sign from Spirit manifested through your higher self, using me as a channel or intended messenger. What's message? "Do your shadow work." Reading this and feeling its resonance is no accident—it's a direct echo of your soul's true desires, delivered on divine timing. The call is here. Loud and clear. It's up to you to listen, follow, ignore, or resist. Free will is yours.

There is another way your higher-self communicates urgency. Sometimes you need a kind yet ruthless, no-filter and no-sugar-coating messenger like me, but sometimes your soul "whispers."

Soul whispers are a complete unfolding. They're different. They don't announce themselves boldly. They emerge as subtle feelings, intuitive nudges, and quiet truths urging us toward our highest potential. When the need for shadow work becomes palpable, there is no more ignoring it.

Free will allows you to listen, follow, ignore, or resist. But when soul whispers turn into persistent patterns of suffering, free will is no longer about resisting—it's about choosing evolution before discomfort forces your hand.

Unlike the critical voice of your ego or the fear-based whispers of doubt, soul whispers feel like a quiet but **certain knowing**—a pull towards expansion, not protection.

The urgent need for shadow work often manifests in ways we don't immediately recognize. It may show up as personal disregard, people-pleasing, or self-sacrifice. Our energy begins to exude an undeniable emptiness. We might experience low self-esteem, lack of confidence, self-sabotage, or an inability to manifest our desires.

We often feel something is missing but can't quite pinpoint what. Life becomes a cycle of struggle—stress, discontentment, disappointment, and lack. Love, happiness, success, or inner peace seem out of reach. Problems, chaos, toxicity, and negativity start accumulating, weighing us down and limiting our growth.

Understanding Patterns, Triggers, and Projections

Shadows reveal themselves as patterns, triggers, and projections, mirroring our void for us to notice. The shadow communicates in this coded way because that is how your subconscious reveals what you're unwilling to face consciously. Recognizing these signs is the first step to reclaiming your power—and with awareness, you can finally choose to break free.

Our soul whispers to be heard through intuition and gut feelings until they become loud cries for help. This escalation can progress from energy and thoughts to feelings, emotions, and even physical manifestations. Depending on our level of awareness, we may or may not notice these constant signs and alarms.

- Can you notice when you are projecting?
- Can you tell when you feel triggered or reactive?
- Have you noticed repetitive patterns or issues in your life?

Sometimes, we're so busy that we overlook these issues as normal parts of life. But they are not! It's our soul helping us identify where love is missing and where healing needs to take place.

Let's dive deeper:

Patterns: Recurring behaviors, thoughts, emotions, or situations that repeatedly manifest in your life. These can be both positive and negative, conscious or unconscious. For example, repeatedly choosing similar types of relationships or partners, consistently reacting to stress with anger or withdrawal, or experiencing the same type of conflict repeatedly. These patterns point to aspects of our shadow because the shadow mirrors itself into your reality to be seen, accepted, and integrated. They keep showing up until you are ready to look at them and break the cycle.

- **Self-Reflection** — What recurring patterns do I notice in my relationships or behaviors?
- **Tip** — Journal about one pattern you have identified, exploring its origins and how it impacts your life. Consider how you can start to break this cycle.

Triggers: External stimuli or internal thoughts that evoke a strong or disproportional reaction, often linked to unresolved past experiences or traumas. Like an alarm or a reminder. For example, feeling intense anger when someone criticizes you, reacting defensively to specific words or actions, or strongly disliking someone's behavior. Recognizing triggers allows us to trace these intense reactions back to their origins, revealing hidden wounds and unresolved emotions.

- **Self-Reflection** — What recent event triggered a strong emotional response in me, and why?
- **Tip** — Reflect on a recent trigger and write about the emotions it brought up. Trace these feelings back to their origins and consider ways to address and heal these underlying issues.

Projections: Unconsciously attributing our own unwanted feelings, thoughts, or traits onto others. When we dislike something in ourselves, we point it out in others. This defense mechanism helps us avoid facing our own shadow aspects. For example, accusing others of being selfish when you struggle with selfish tendencies yourself, judging someone as untrustworthy due to your own issues with trust, or seeing others as overly critical while denying your own inner critic.

- **Self-Reflection:** In what ways might I be projecting my own issues onto others?

- **Tip:** Identify a recent instance where you judged someone harshly. Reflect on how this judgment might be a projection of your own inner struggles. Work on developing self-awareness and compassion to reduce judgment and conflict.

Every time you notice a pattern, identify a trigger, or acknowledge a projection, you reclaim more of yourself. This deepens your self-awareness, fuels personal growth, and leads to a more authentic and fulfilling life.

JOURNEY WITHIN: DYNAMICS OF SHADOW WORK

 Know Thyself : Introspections 022-024

22. Triggers: When I feel deeply triggered, what hidden wound or unmet need might be surfacing for healing?

23. Projections: What traits or behaviors in others frustrate or disturb me the most, and how might they reflect something within myself that I haven't fully acknowledged or accepted?

24. Patterns: What recurring experiences, relationships, or emotional cycles keep showing up in my life, and what might they be trying to teach me?

SECTION 11. DIVINE INTERVENTION

Shadow work can be initiated voluntarily or involuntarily, but when we avoid it or resist it, the universe may step in through divine intervention. This occurs when a higher power directly influences human affairs, often through profound realizations, life-altering events, synchronicities, or even drastic upheavals. It serves as a course correction, ensuring that we align with our soul contract, life purpose, and divine calling.

Divine intervention is often perceived as extraordinary acts or events orchestrated by a divine being to guide, assist, or correct individuals or events. It manifests when we continuously ignore soul whispers and shadow manifestations.

Avoidance of shadow work leads to stagnation, spiritual misalignment, shadow-self embodiment, and detachment from our authentic essence. This can compromise not just our personal evolution but also the greater mission we are meant to fulfill. If our work, presence, or purpose is crucial to the collective, intervention becomes inevitable. The universe will disrupt, dismantle, and redirect our lives to ensure that we step into our role. In simple terms, divine intervention helps us get our shift together.

This intervention manifests through guidance, protection, unique messages, signs, serendipity, or miraculous events. It reinforces the idea that humans are not alone and that a divine force is always present, guiding and supporting their journey. However, this also raises questions about free will and how much of our lives are predetermined, so

JOURNEY WITHIN: DYNAMICS OF SHADOW WORK

it's important to highlight here that while divine intervention redirects us, free will remains—how we respond to the intervention determines our growth and path.

Divine intervention manifests uniquely for each soul, but those aligned with a sacred mission often experience the most profound shifts. Some souls are "marked" or "chosen" for a mission that is integral to the greater good. When such individuals refuse to awaken, their avoidance delays or derails not only their destiny but the collective evolution. The universe cannot allow this. Those who carry sacred contracts—healers, teachers, guides, and way-showers—are often the ones who experience the most intense interventions.

We always have a choice. We can consciously engage in shadow work, acknowledging and addressing our projections, triggers, and patterns before intervention becomes necessary. Proactive inner work prevents the need for harsh corrections, allowing us to evolve with grace rather than struggle. But when we resist, the universe will intervene—not as punishment, but as an act of divine grace and compassion—to ensure we assume our role and fulfill our highest calling.

SECTION 12. A 'TOWER MOMENT'

Ignoring our soul whispers and the urgent call to confront our inner shadows can lead to profound and transformative experiences, often referred to as "tower moments" and "dark nights of the soul." These experiences are co-created by our higher self in alignment with a higher power.

Tower Moments can be self-inflicted or divinely initiated. Self-inflicted ones arise when we repeatedly ignore warnings, deny truth, or refuse necessary growth—forcing the collapse of what no longer serves. Divinely initiated Tower Moments, however, are cosmic interventions designed to propel us into alignment when we've strayed too far from our soul's path.

In Tarot, a "tower moment" is symbolized by the Tower card, depicting a tower struck by lightning, causing its destruction. This card represents sudden upheaval, unexpected change, and the breakdown of old structures or beliefs.

Tower moments dismantle false foundations, forcing transformation that leads to greater alignment, resilience, and clarity. These intense experiences force us to face the shadows we've been avoiding, leading to profound personal and spiritual transformation.

A Tower Moment feels like everything is falling apart at once—unexpected losses, abrupt endings, or emotional upheavals that demand immediate change. If life suddenly feels like a storm without shelter, you may be in the midst of one.

Often, we don't recognize a Tower Moment in real time; it feels chaotic and disorienting. Only in hindsight do we see its purpose. They bring about disruption, forced reflection, inner critic confrontation, the death of the ego, soul purification, spiritual awakening, and life rebuilding.

SECTION 13. DARK NIGHT OF THE SOUL

The Dark Night of the Soul is a profound spiritual and existential crisis where an individual experiences intense feelings of disconnection, despair, and inner turmoil. It is often triggered by a major life event, deep self-inquiry, or a spiritual awakening that forces one to confront their shadow, illusions, and ego-based attachments.

The Dark Night of the Soul extends beyond the Tower Moment, dismantling internal foundations at the deepest level.

While a Tower Moment shatters illusions and external structures, the Dark Night of the Soul dismantles internal foundations—beliefs, identity, and perceived meaning—forcing a deep, unavoidable reckoning.

This phase often follows a Tower Moment as one struggles to process its aftermath. Many will experience multiple Dark Nights, each refining the soul at different levels of consciousness. It can arise from ignoring soul whispers, resisting transformation, attempting to rebuild old structures, or overriding divine intervention with free will. When the ego clings to what has already crumbled, the soul intervenes, dragging the individual into the depths of their own shadow.

The Dark Night of the Soul is an unavoidable initiation in deep shadow work. It strips away illusions, compels confrontation with hidden wounds, and exposes unconscious patterns that no longer serve. The process is painful, disorienting, and isolating, but it is also a profound catalyst for self-realization. Through surrender and integration, one emerges with greater clarity, wisdom, and alignment with their higher self—reborn into deeper authenticity and spiritual sovereignty.

Key Aspects of the Dark Night of the Soul:

- **Loss of Meaning & Identity** — A feeling of being lost, questioning one's purpose, beliefs, and reality.

- **Ego Death** — Old aspects of the self crumbles, leading to confusion and emotional suffering.

- **Emotional & Spiritual Purging** — Deep-rooted fears, traumas, and suppressed emotions rise to the surface.

- **Isolation & Loneliness** — A perceived disconnection, meant to strip external attachments and guide one inward toward true connection.

- **Transformation & Rebirth** — If navigated properly, this leads to greater self-awareness, spiritual enlightenment, and alignment with one's authentic self.

ILLUMINATION
Tower Moment vs. Divine Intervention vs. Dark Night of the Soul

These three experiences—Tower Moments, Divine Intervention, and the Dark Night of the Soul—are disruptive dynamics yet deeply transformational. While they share similarities, they differ in cause, intensity, and purpose.

Divine Intervention (Guided Disruption & Alignment)

Before a Tower Moment or a Dark Night of the Soul unfolds, Divine Intervention often steps in as a guiding force—sometimes subtle, sometimes unmistakable.

- **What it is:** A higher force stepping in to realign your path, often through synchronicities, signs, or unexpected redirections.
- **Cause:** The Universe intervening when you're misaligned with your soul's purpose.
- **Experience:** Redirection, miracles, blessings in disguise, feeling "pushed" toward necessary change.
- **Purpose:** To remove obstacles, open doors, and course-correct your journey before a greater upheaval becomes necessary.

Understanding Universe's Intervention

Free will allows us to make choices, including resisting growth or change. However, every choice carries consequences. When we resist the flow of our soul's journey or sacred mission, we create stagnation, blocks, or misalignment. The Universe's "intervention" isn't about bullying or forcing us, but about presenting opportunities to realign with our highest path.

Divine Intervention can be gentle nudges or drastic shifts, depending on how much we resist. Ignoring these signs often escalates into a Tower Moment.

Imagine the Universe as a loving guide rather than an enforcer. Its interventions are like those of a wise teacher (or a loving but firm parent) who sees our potential and refuses to let us settle for less. While it respects our free will, it also ensures we don't lose ourselves in the noise of fear, denial, or inertia. What feels like "intervention" is often the Universe responding to our deeper, unspoken desire for change. It is not challenging us arbitrarily—it is mirroring our higher self's intention to evolve.

The Fool's Journey, for example, reminds us that resisting our soul's purpose doesn't erase it—it only amplifies the call. The longer we delay, the louder it becomes. When gentle nudges are ignored, the Universe shifts from subtle signs to unmistakable disruptions. This is how The Fool—once wandering in innocence—becomes the Hero and evolves into The Fool 2.0: a version of self that walks the path of wisdom, armed with conviction, self-knowledge, and resilience.

And when resistance reaches its peak, Divine Intervention often manifests as a Tower Moment—a sudden, unavoidable collapse of everything misaligned, forcing us to face the truth we've been avoiding.

Tower Moment (Sudden Collapse & Disruption)

A Tower Moment happens when illusions and external structures collapse, forcing rapid transformation. If Divine Intervention is the Universe whispering, a Tower Moment is the Universe shouting.

- **What it is:** A sudden, unexpected event that shakes your foundation—loss, betrayal, drastic change, or a harsh realization.
- **Cause:** Often triggered by external forces or ignored inner truths reaching a breaking point.
- **Experience:** Shock, chaos, emotional upheaval, ego destruction.
- **Purpose:** To break down false structures, illusions, and stagnation so that you can rebuild on truth.

Tower Moments can be self-inflicted (from avoidance and resistance) or divinely initiated (a cosmic push toward necessary growth). Recognizing a Tower Moment while it's happening can offer clarity—many only realize it in hindsight.

There is no set order: A Divine Intervention can lead to a Tower Moment, or a Tower Moment can trigger a Divine Intervention. But if the inner crisis deepens, it may evolve into a Dark Night of the Soul.

DARK NIGHT OF THE SOUL
(Existential Crisis & Spiritual Death/Rebirth)

The Dark Night of the Soul is an intensified evolution of a Tower Moment, plunging an individual into profound spiritual desolation, disconnection, and existential crisis. While a Tower Moment dismantles external structures, the Dark Night of the Soul dismantles the internal self—beliefs, identity, and perceived meaning.

- **What it is:** A deep spiritual and existential crisis where you feel disconnected from yourself, others, and even the Divine.
- **Cause:** An internal awakening process, where the old self dissolves to make way for a new, higher self.
- **Experience:** Despair, emotional purging, feeling lost, loss of meaning, questioning everything.
- **Purpose:** To strip away illusions, ego attachments, and deep-rooted fears, leading to self-realization and spiritual evolution.

Neglecting the shadow self can manifest as emotional, mental, spiritual, physical, behavioral, social, and interpersonal challenges. It creates blockages, stagnation, and long-term consequences such as spiritual bypassing and the erosion of authenticity.

Though painful, the Dark Night of the Soul is a sacred opportunity. When we surrender to the process, we emerge not only with greater clarity and wisdom but also with a deeper connection to our true essence—reborn, sovereign, and aligned with our highest path.

In summary:

- Divine Intervention redirects your path before chaos unfolds.
- A Tower Moment shatters illusions and external stability.
- The Dark Night of the Soul dismantles the internal self, leading to transformation.
- Ignoring soul whispers prolongs suffering—resistance amplifies the upheaval.

When faced with these experiences, the choice is always ours: embrace the transformation or resist and prolong the inevitable.

PHASE II
Turning Inward

Healing is not a straight path. It twists, loops, and sometimes doubles back before moving forward. Before we fully commit to transformation, it's natural to resist. Rejection is often part of acceptance. The call to heal can feel overwhelming, inconvenient, or even threatening to the identity we've built. We may deny it, bargain with it, or delay the inevitable.

But detours are not failures. They are part of the process. Some reject the call because healing requires surrender, and surrender feels like losing control. Others fear what they will uncover if they turn inward. Yet, the call does not disappear—it lingers, waiting for us to be ready. The more we resist, the more the call will return, louder each time, until we have no choice but to face ourselves.

Sometimes we know what needs to be done, yet something stops us, triggering a fight, flight, freeze, or fawn response. This hesitation isn't just resistance—it's self-preservation. The mind and body perceive change as a threat to stability, even when the current reality is unhealthy or unfulfilling.

For example, someone stuck in a toxic relationship may know they need to leave, yet fear of abandonment, financial insecurity, or uncertainty about the future keeps them paralyzed. A person who desperately wants to heal from childhood wounds might sign up for therapy but cancel the first session because facing the past feels too overwhelming. An entrepreneur with a vision may delay launching their business out of fear of failure or judgment, convincing themselves they need "just a little more time" to prepare.

These moments of hesitation aren't just procrastination—they're nervous system responses trying to keep us "safe" in the familiar. But safety isn't always aligned with growth. Recognizing when we are stuck in self-protective avoidance is the first step toward moving forward.

One of my personal hardships, part of my Call to Adventure, was accepting my sexual identity. And it was beyond obvious and clear, but I felt like I was trying to cover the Sun with one finger. I will share more with you in the next chapters as we navigate the Journey Within, but long story short I knew I had to eventually come out of the closet, but there was always an excuse to prolong the timing. It wasn't that I didn't want to come out—it was that I first needed to come out to myself.

The awareness was there. The realization was palpable. The soul whispers weren't just whispers; they were screaming—no pun intended. And yet, I stayed. The analysis paralysis and the fear about the "adjustments" needed to be made and the "explaining" or the "judgment" that follows this sort of admission was not in my top 3 to do. Excuses, after excuses. Meanwhile my soul' spark was vanishing.

Inside the closet, I felt an emptiness that words can barely describe. A hollow existence where I performed rather than lived. The lack of authenticity bled into everything—my creativity, my relationships, my presence in the world. I was showing up, but not fully. I was speaking, but not truthfully. I was existing, but not living. There was a disconnect between who I was on the inside and how I allowed myself to be seen. That split drained me. It kept me small, hesitant, and incomplete.

It wasn't the fear of rejection that paralyzed me the most—it was the fear of my own radiance. The fear of standing fully in my truth, of embodying all that I knew myself to be. I hesitated, I procrastinated, I rationalized. And in doing so, I unknowingly invited divine intervention. The universe doesn't wait forever. My avoidance was met with a Tower Moment—one that shattered the illusion of safety I had built around myself. Looking back, I realize that the very thing I feared—myself in my fullest expression—was the key to my liberation.

Accepting the call is not about having no fear. It's about choosing growth despite it. It's about recognizing that avoidance only prolongs suffering and that the true path to wholeness begins the moment we stop running and turn inward.

HERO'S MILESTONE 3
Refusing the Call

In our Journey Within, Sanctuary represents devotion to self—answering the call and turning inward to care for our soul's need for healing. This is self-care in its deepest form. Yet, inner conflict, self-doubt, resistance, and fear often arise when The Call to Adventure is heard.

This resistance can be rooted in:

- A fear of failure or change
- An attachment to comfort zones and the familiar
- The belief that the challenges ahead are too great to overcome

These fears are not random; they are conditioned responses. The ego thrives on predictability, seeking safety in the familiar—even if the familiar is limiting or painful. When faced with the unknown, the mind rationalizes avoidance, numbs discomfort, or dismisses the need for transformation. The journey remains necessary, but resistance makes it more painful.

The Universe Always Calls—The Choice is Ours

The Fool's Journey is not just about adventure—it is an invitation to inner growth, shadow integration, and self-realization. Ignoring this summons does not remove the path;

it only delays it, prompting the Universe to intervene. Disruptions, losses, and upheavals arise—not as punishments, but as realignments. Nudges to push The Fool back on track toward their destined path.

These nudges begin as whispers but intensify when ignored.

When The Fool answers the call, transformation begins. Acceptance disrupts the status quo and requires a leap into the unknown. This is the turning point where The Fool steps beyond fear and initiates true growth.

The Journey Requires:

- **Stepping into The Unknown** — Moving beyond comfort zones and embracing new experiences.
- **Confronting the Shadow** — Facing hidden fears, self-doubt, and limiting beliefs.
- **Acquiring Wisdom & Tools** — Learning from mentors, guides, and lessons (both external and internal).
- **Transformation** — Shedding outdated identities, integrating the shadow, and embodying a more self-aware, empowered version of self.
- **Expansion of Consciousness** — Opening to new awareness, deeper intuition, and alignment with purpose.

Answering the call is an act of courage—one that leads to growth, healing, and a deeper connection with the higher self.

Why Does The Fool Reject the Call?

- **Fear of the Unknown:** The Fool's innocence often leads to a fear of uncertainty or stepping outside their comfort zone, making the leap forward seem daunting.

- **Ego Resistance:** The ego craves certainty, and transformation demands the surrender of control. The mind whispers, "You're fine where you are," or "You're not capable of what lies ahead," fostering complacency or doubt.

- **Denial of Inner Truth:** Growth requires facing hidden fears, flaws, and truths. The Fool may unconsciously resist not only discomfort but the responsibility that comes with self-awareness. Accepting the call means embracing their power—and with power comes accountability.

Consequences of Refusing the Call:

- **The Shadow Grows Louder:** Suppressed fears, insecurities, and unresolved wounds intensify, often manifesting as anxiety, emptiness, depression, or discontent. The Fool's shadow self—the hidden or denied aspects of self—demands attention, creating mental, emotional, spiritual, and even physical turmoil. Chronic fatigue, restlessness, or unexplained illnesses can emerge as the body carries the weight of unresolved inner conflict.

- **Stagnation:** Without embracing change, The Fool remains trapped in a repetitive, unfulfilling loop. Relationships, careers, and personal aspirations suffer from a lack of depth and authenticity. What once felt comfortable begins to feel suffocating.

- **Divine Intervention:** When resistance persists, the universe steps in with Tower Moments—events that force transformation through loss, heartbreak, or upheaval. These are not punishments but cosmic recalibrations, stripping away illusions and false securities to reveal the truth. This is the equivalent of The Fool being "pushed off the cliff" they refused to leap from.

- **Recurring Patterns:** The rejected call returns with greater intensity, creating karmic lessons and challenges until The Fool steps forward. The Universe repeats lessons with increasing urgency until integration occurs. Each cycle is a new opportunity to step into alignment.

The Call Always Awaits

Ultimately, every Fool reaches a crossroads: surrender to stagnation or embrace the adventure of self-evolution. The call remains, waiting for the moment we decide to answer.

JOURNEY WITHIN DOORWAY #2.
The Sanctuary (Devotion to Self)

If we are fortunate enough to heed the call, we step into a Sanctuary—a sacred space within where we commit to shadow work and the journey inward. This is devotion to self, the act of claiming our worth and nurturing our authentic being. Here, we unravel and confront our shadows, honoring their lessons while releasing their limitations. It is in this space that we rekindle the flame of self-discovery and reconnect with our truest essence.

Sanctuary symbolizes our commitment to self-healing, self-discovery, and self-empowerment—a metaphorical and spiritual refuge where we nurture our soul, engage in inner work, and embrace transformation.

It is the embodiment of self-devotion, a conscious choice to honor our worth, cultivate authenticity, and prioritize personal growth. Within this sacred space, we cultivate inner peace, safety, and deep alignment with our higher self.

I want you to connect with this: Sanctuary happens when we no longer run from ourselves.

It is the moment we stop fearing the unknown and start trusting that within self-care and devotion to self lies our liberation. It is a choice to meet ourselves fully, to sit with what we once rejected, and to reclaim every part of our being. The call to look inward stops feeling like an imposition and starts feeling like an invitation. It is no longer about fixing but remembering and becoming.

Readiness for devotion is a nudge from within. A feeling like no other. But what exactly shifts within us that make us feel ready to go inward?

Catalyst Shakes Us Awake (The big shakeup)

Sometimes, we do not walk willingly into shadow work—it pulls us in. A life event cracks us open, leaving us with no choice but to face what we've been avoiding.

How It Feels:

- A loss, betrayal, or ending forces deep reflection.
- Old wounds, trauma, or conditioning surface in ways we cannot ignore.
- A profound sense of misalignment or existential questioning arises.

These moments serve as initiations, revealing that healing is not just about recovery—it is about reclamation.

Avoidance Becomes More Painful Than the Truth (The resistance collapses)

We reach a point where denial, distraction, or suppression no longer hold. The weight of our shadows becomes too heavy to carry, and we recognize that turning inward is not just an option—it is the only way forward.

How It Feels:

- Cycles of pain repeat until we cannot ignore them.
- External validation or coping mechanisms no longer provide relief.
- We feel exhausted by the effort of pretending.

- There is an unshakable knowing that change must come from within.

This is when shadow work ceases to be a distant concept and becomes a necessity.

We Feel Held—By Ourselves, Another, or the Universe *(Realizing we are not alone)*

Safety is not the absence of difficulty, but the presence of support. This support may come from within, from a trusted guide, or from the invisible hands of the Universe reminding us that we are not alone.

How It Manifests:

- Self-compassion: We stop abandoning or shaming ourselves.
- A guiding presence: A mentor, therapist, or soul connection offers space for our process.
- Divine reassurance: A felt sense that we are being led, that the timing is right.

When we sense that we are supported, the fear of facing ourselves begins to dissolve.

Curiosity Replaces Fear (A new lens emerges)

There is a subtle yet profound shift when we stop seeing our shadows as enemies and start recognizing them as messengers. The work no longer feels like a punishment—it becomes an opportunity.

How This Shift Feels:

- Instead of "Why is this happening to me?" we ask, "What is this teaching me?"
- We feel drawn to self-reflection, journaling, or deeper conversations.
- We notice synchronicities guiding us inward.

Curiosity invites us to explore without judgment, making shadow work feel less like diving into darkness and more like retrieving lost pieces of ourselves.

The Soul's Whisper Becomes Too Loud to Ignore
(The final surrender)

Long before we act, our soul whispers to us. It speaks through intuition, dreams, and gentle nudges—urging us toward truth. We may resist at first, but eventually, the whispers become undeniable.

How the Soul Calls Us Inward:

- Recurring dreams, symbols, or visions.
- Sudden emotional triggers demanding attention.
- A feeling of disconnection from our true self.
- A deep, unshakable knowing that something must shift.

When we finally listen, we realize that shadow work is not about fixing what is broken—it is about remembering who we are.

HERO'S MILESTONE 4
Accepting the Call

The Fool eventually accepts the Call. The Fool 2.0 only emerges once the call is finally answered, typically after experiencing humbling, awakening, or being forced into action.

Even after rejection, The Fool's Journey is far from over. Rejection may delay the journey, but it doesn't derail it permanently. The Universe is patient yet persistent, always finding ways to bring The Fool back to their path, no matter how far they stray.

Speaking of humbling, I needed a reality check to realize that I wasn't in control at all. I had to confront the truth that not only was I off track, but I was also on the verge of derailing from my sacred path. Over time, my panic attacks escalated. What started as rare occurrences became monthly, then weekly, and eventually almost daily, often culminating in visits to the ER.

During one visit, the doctor told me there was nothing wrong with my heart, stomach, or nervous system. "Everything is fine!" he said. With a deep compassionate gaze, he asked, "Why are you really here?" For the first time, I felt truly seen and yet so exposed. Then, with a warm smile, he asked, "Have you ever considered therapy?"

He suggested CBT (cognitive behavior therapy)—a type of psychotherapy that helps people manage mental and physical health issues by changing thought patterns and behaviors. He also mentioned that my sensitivity to sounds, lights, smells, food, and social environments seemed similar to someone on the autism spectrum. "I think it's time for you to not suffer anymore," he said. "You can make it go away," he emphasized.

At first, I was "shook" by this suggestion and even indignant at the idea of seeing a "shrink," but over time, I realized his message was another form of divine intervention. Despite my initial reaction, his words lingered in my mind for weeks, and I found myself reflecting deeply. He had answered the question that had plagued me for so long: Why was my experience of life so complex and painful?

For the first time, I saw how my spiritual sensitivities and neurodivergence intertwined—how my heightened perception, my deep emotional landscape, and my struggles weren't just mystical gifts or ethereal notions but also deeply human realities. I was a human being on the autistic spectrum, undiagnosed and suffering, doing the best I could. And that realization broke my heart.

Imagine judging a child—a baby girl—calling her a weirdo, criticizing her for feeling sick in crowds, mocking her struggle to connect with others, or picking on her for having a sensitive stomach—only to later realize she had a real condition all along. That's how I felt I had been treating myself. For the first time ever, I truly felt sorry for myself—for the child within me who had been so often dismissed.

So, I decided to take his advice and sought help from a spiritual therapist who offered a holistic approach that resonated with me. She focused on helping me navigate self-awareness. Yes, the ER doctor planted the seed, but

it was ultimately my decision to seek healing, to love myself enough to confront my truth, that catalyzed my transformation.
I decided to answer the call.
"Hello, shadow work. Have we met before?"

Know Thyself: Introspections 025

25. The Sanctuary: What practices or intentions can I dedicate myself to nurture my inner world and honor my healing journey?

DIVINE INTERVENTION

- **The Tower** — Sudden upheaval, destruction of false foundations.
- **Death** — Endings that must happen for transformation to occur.
- **10 of Swords** — Rock bottom, betrayal, deep surrender.
- **Judgement** — Karmic reckoning, self-accountability, spiritual awakening.

CHAPTER THREE
PREPARATION

Accepting the Call vs. Being Prepared

Realization is the spark, but preparation is the foundation that allows transformation to unfold with greater ease.

Shadow work often begins with a moment of clarity—an awakening to patterns, emotions, or wounds that are ready to be explored. This realization is a powerful invitation to healing. However, being *aware* that change is needed and being *prepared* to navigate that change are two different things.

Accepting the call means saying *yes* to your growth. Preparation means giving yourself the care, tools, and support to walk this path with confidence. It's not about perfection or knowing exactly what lies ahead—it's about *building trust in yourself* and approaching your journey with intention.

Shadow work doesn't require that you have everything figured out; it only asks that you meet yourself where you are and take one conscious step at a time.

What Does It Mean to Be Prepared?

Preparation is not about pressure or rigidity. It's about creating a space where you feel *safe, supported, and empowered* to explore your inner world. This involves caring for yourself in three key areas:

- **A Prepared Mind —** The mind is where doubt and resistance can arise. Preparation here means cultivating curiosity instead of fear, setting intentions, and creating small, manageable steps that keep you moving forward.

- **A Nurtured Body** — Your body holds emotions, memories, and energy. Supporting it through movement, rest, and nourishment ensures you feel grounded and strong as you engage in shadow work.

- **An Anchored Spirit** — Your spirit is your inner compass, guiding you toward your truth. Whether through meditation, journaling, or moments of stillness, strengthening this connection allows you to approach the journey with greater trust and ease.

The Power of Preparation: Easing into the Journey

Stepping into shadow work is not about bracing for impact—it's about creating a *gentle landing* for yourself. Preparation ensures that as thoughts, memories, feelings and emotions rise, you have the tools to hold yourself with care. It reminds you that this work is not about battling your darkness, but about embracing all parts of you with compassion.

Preparation also keeps you steady, preventing you from rushing in without direction. However, you don't need to be perfectly ready—you just need to be willing. This chapter will guide you through simple, supportive ways to prepare so that as you take your first steps, you do so feeling held, empowered, and deeply supported by yourself.

SECTION 14. SIGNIFICANCE

- *What would it mean to you to live a life where your past no longer controls you, and you are fully aligned with your true power?*
- *What would be possible if you stood unapologetically in your truth, free from fear, doubt, or the need for validation?*
- *How would it feel to embrace a life where abundance flows effortlessly, unblocked by unworthiness or limitation? or experiencing love and a deep relationship that is free from fear, self-sabotage, or past wounds—where you can give and receive fully, without hesitation?*

Only you can define what holds meaning, value, and impact in your life.

Establishing significance is the art of discerning what is truly meaningful and worth claiming in your life. It is the process of recognizing what aligns with your deepest values, purpose, and truth—then choosing to nurture, protect, and cultivate it with intention. What holds significance is not just what feels important in the moment but what contributes to your growth, fulfillment, and self-mastery. It requires clarity, commitment, and the willingness to invest in what truly matters while releasing what does not. In defining significance, you define the foundation upon which your power, prosperity, love, and purpose thrive.

The significance of shadow work lies in its power to transform your life and manifest your true heart's desires. The journey within—the deep dive into our inner landscape—is the bridge between our inner and outer worlds. It impacts not only our personal well-being but also how we engage with the collective. Through this process, we uncover the unseen influences shaping our thoughts, behaviors, energy, emotional responses, and spiritual processes, allowing us to reclaim our authenticity.

Identifying Areas for Healing

Recognizing what needs healing is the first step in transformation. Shadow work reveals the hidden influences that shape our emotions, beliefs, and behaviors. Begin by reflecting on the areas in your life that feel heavy or misaligned

To begin shadow work, reflect on the areas of your life that feel misaligned or weighed down. Reflect on aspects of your life that have room for improvement or could use a reset.

Consider:

- What emotions or patterns keep surfacing?
- Where do you feel blocked, stagnant, or unfulfilled?
- How would your life change if you felt free from limiting beliefs and past wounds?

Healing isn't just about past traumas; it's also about building coping mechanisms and navigating present challenges – like self-doubt, rejection, social conditioning, anxiety, and burnout. By working through these, we free up energy that can be redirected into our highest potential.

Expanding Intuition, Self-Trust, and Personal Sovereignty

Engaging in shadow work strengthens three core aspects of self-mastery: intuition, self-trust, and personal sovereignty. These qualities form the foundation of authentic living, allowing you to navigate life with clarity, confidence, and autonomy.

Strengthening Intuition

Intuition is the deep, inner knowing that guides us beyond logic and external influences. However, when unhealed wounds, suppressed emotions, and societal conditioning cloud our inner landscape, it becomes difficult to distinguish intuition from fear, doubt, or conditioning.

Shadow work clears these distortions by bringing unconscious patterns to light. As you release limiting beliefs and past programming, your intuitive voice becomes clearer and more accessible. You start recognizing the difference between gut instincts and trauma responses, between authentic knowing and conditioned fears.

Through self-inquiry, emotional processing, and integration, you begin to **trust your inner voice** rather than constantly seeking validation from external sources. This allows you to move through life with greater discernment, recognizing what truly aligns with you versus what is rooted in societal or relational conditioning.

Deepening Self-Trust

Self-trust is the ability to rely on yourself—to know that you will show up for yourself no matter what. Many struggle with self-trust due to past betrayals (by self or others), fear of making mistakes, or external influences that have made them doubt their worth and capabilities.

Shadow work restores self-trust by helping you understand why you second-guess yourself, where self-doubt originates, and how to reclaim your inner authority. When you face your fears, insecurities, and wounds head-on, you prove to yourself that you are capable of holding and healing your own experiences.

Each time you move through discomfort instead of avoiding it, you reinforce self-trust. You learn that you are resilient, that you can handle your emotions, and that your feelings are valid. Over time, this cultivates a deep, unshakable trust in yourself, allowing you to make decisions with confidence, set boundaries with conviction, and honor your needs without guilt.

Reclaiming Personal Sovereignty

I'm big on this one. I call it "Peacock" mode.

It's an organic level of confidence that comes not from ego, but from embracing our inner strength.

When you step into this energy and embrace your inner Peacock, you no longer shrink to make others comfortable. Your energy radiates effortlessly—because true confidence isn't performed, it's embodied.

JOURNEY WITHIN: DYNAMICS OF SHADOW WORK

And guess what? It looks damn good on you.

Personal sovereignty is the ability to govern yourself—emotionally, mentally, and energetically—without being controlled by external forces, past traumas, or societal expectations. It means standing firmly in your truth, making choices aligned with your highest self, and owning your power <u>unapologetically</u>.

Through shadow work, you break free from old programming that kept you in cycles of people-pleasing, self-sacrifice, or self-sabotage. You reclaim your right to define yourself, rather than letting others dictate who you should be. This level of self-ownership allows you to move through the world with confidence, autonomy, and an unwavering sense of self.

When intuition, self-trust, and sovereignty work in harmony, you no longer seek permission to exist as your fullest expression. You become the conscious creator of your reality, aligned with your truth, purpose, and power.

SECTION 15. OPENNESS AND READINESS TO HEAL

Approaching shadow work with openness is key. Resistance is natural, but when we move through it with curiosity rather than avoidance, we unlock deeper layers of healing. The more receptive and engaged you are, the more profound and lasting your transformation will be.

Healing requires courage, commitment, and self-trust. This path is not one of self-punishment but of self-liberation. Shadow work allows you to reclaim the parts of yourself that have been hidden, suppressed, or wounded. By embracing this process, you step into greater authenticity, balance, and inner peace.

However, openness alone is not enough. Readiness is the bridge between intention and action. It means not just wanting to heal but actively preparing for it—mentally, emotionally, and spiritually. Without readiness, resistance can create stagnation and hinder progress. But when you cultivate an open heart and an accepting mindset, you allow transformation to flow with more ease.

OVERCOMING RESISTANCE:
Reframing Fear as Part of Readiness

It's human nature to fear the unknown, especially when it resides within us. Imagine standing at the entrance of a dark cave—uncertain, hesitant. This is how shadow work may feel. But remember, you are not entering blindly. Accessing your innermost will never feel like entering a "dark cave of doom." You have a flashlight—your awareness, intention, and the tools needed to navigate this journey safely.

Fear and discomfort often manifest as procrastination, avoidance, or self-sabotage. Acknowledge this without judgment. Instead of viewing resistance as a roadblock, see it as an indicator of growth. You are stepping into a space where deep transformation is possible.

It's natural to feel a bit apprehensive at first but try to reframe this inner quest as a heartfelt conversation with your closest friend. You wouldn't judge or criticize them for their vulnerabilities—you would be kind, supportive, and compassionate. Well, you deserve the same treatment from yourself.

Steps to Cultivate Readiness & Openness

1. **Establish Its Significance** — Anchor yourself in why you're doing shadow work. Focus on the bigger picture and your desired outcome. Understanding its importance will help you stay committed and motivated. Clarity of purpose fuels readiness.

2. **Acknowledge Your Emotions** — It's completely normal to feel apprehensive about shadow work. Instead of resisting your emotions, embrace them with curiosity, love, respect, and understanding. Recognize that this journey is an act of courage, leading you toward self-awareness, growth, and self-mastery.

3. **Give Yourself Credit** — Bravery isn't about the absence of fear; it's about moving forward despite it. Recognize your strength in choosing this path. Every step you take, no matter how small, is an act of resilience and empowerment.

4. **Create a Safe Space** — Set aside a dedicated space and time for your practice. Ensure you're in an environment where you feel safe and supported—whether it's a cozy corner, a quiet spot in nature, or a sacred space designed for introspection and healing.

5. **Start Small** — Take small, intentional steps. Shadow work doesn't have to be overwhelming. You can start with manageable reflections or journaling prompts. Give yourself permission to go at your own pace. Build confidence by exploring deeper layers gradually. Honor your own pace, there's no rush or pressure, and taking breaks is perfectly okay.

6. **Find a Support System** — You don't have to do this alone. Whether you prefer a solo, self-paced journey or coach-guided program, surround yourself with supportive tools, experts, and communities. Having a structure can keep you accountable and supported. Seek out resources that keep you focused and inspired.

Always remember: you are enough, your efforts matter, and the only validation you need is yours. If you're looking for a safe space to start, consider exploring our **One Vessel** community—we're here for you every step of the way.

7. **Cultivate Self-Compassion** — Be kind to yourself. Acknowledge any fears or resistance without judgment. Shadow work requires patience, and you deserve the same love and compassion you'd offer a dear friend. Reassure yourself that you're capable of facing and integrating your shadow aspects with acceptance. And most importantly, celebrate every victory—no matter how small.

8. **Celebrate Your Progress** — Acknowledge each moment of self-awareness and growth. Every step forward, no matter how small, is a victory.

Having embraced openness and readiness to heal, the next step is to move forward with intention.

Shadow work is not just about what we uncover—it's about what we choose to do with it. As we develop openness and readiness, the next step is setting clear intentions for our healing journey. Intentions guide us, ensuring that our transformation is purposeful, sustainable, and aligned with our highest self.

SECTION 16. SETTING CLEAR INTENTIONS

By setting conscious, focused intentions, we create a guiding light that illuminates the path ahead.

Intentions are the conscious and deliberate commitments we make about how we want to direct our energy, thoughts, and actions. They serve as guiding principles that shape our choices, behaviors, and overall path. Unlike goals, which focus on a specific outcome, intentions are about alignment with our values, purpose, and desired way of being.

Why It's Important to Clarify and Define Our Intentions

1. **Provides Clarity and Direction** — Without clear intentions, we risk wandering aimlessly or making decisions that don't align with our highest self. When we define our intentions, we create a roadmap that helps us stay focused and purposeful.

2. **Aligns Energy and Actions** — Intentions ensure that our energy and actions are moving in the same direction. When we are intentional, we operate with mindfulness and alignment, making it easier to manifest what we truly desire.

3. **Strengthens Commitment and Accountability** — Defining our intentions creates a sense of personal responsibility. It encourages us to stay committed to our journey and hold ourselves accountable for the energy we put into the world.

4. **Shapes Our Reality** — Our thoughts, emotions, and beliefs influence our experiences. When we set clear intentions, we consciously shape our reality rather than being controlled by subconscious patterns or external influences.

5. **Supports Emotional and Spiritual Growth** — Clarifying our intentions allows us to move through life with awareness and purpose. It deepens self-awareness, helping us recognize what truly matters and release what no longer serves us.

6. **Prevents Distractions and Misalignment** — Without well-defined intentions, we may find ourselves easily distracted by external expectations, societal pressures, or other people's agendas. Setting clear intentions helps us stay true to ourselves.

7. **Enhances Manifestation and Creation** — When we are intentional, we send a powerful message to the universe about what we are calling in. It strengthens our ability to manifest and co-create our reality.

In shadow work, establishing clear intentions is crucial because it ensures that our healing journey is purposeful, conscious, and aligned with our personal evolution. Instead of blindly reacting to triggers or past wounds, we engage with our shadows with the intention to heal, integrate, and transform.

PREPARATION

Preparing for the Journey Ahead

The following Know Thyself shadow kit introspections are designed to help you:

- **Set a Strong Foundation** — Establish clarity, purpose, and alignment for your shadow work journey.

- **Address Fears & Challenges** — Identify and navigate any emotional resistance or limiting beliefs that may arise.

- **Gather Essential Tools, Resources & Support** — Equip yourself with the knowledge, guidance, and community needed for sustainable growth.

- **Maintain Accountability** — Stay committed to your journey by tracking your actions and intentions.

- **Monitor Progress, Expansion & Impact** — Reflect on your growth, transformation, and the influence of your work on yourself and others.

- **Ensure Integration & Embodiment** — Internalize your lessons and apply them in daily life, allowing your healing and self-mastery to become a lived experience.

E-COURSE LECTURE: "Unlocking Possibility"

**Know Thyself: Introspections 026-061
For Clarifying Intention**

SETTING THE FOUNDATION

26. What is my primary intention for embarking on this shadow work journey, and why is it important at this stage of my life?

27. What are my ultimate goals and desired outcomes for engaging in shadow work?

28. What specific areas of my life do I feel are lacking or need improvement?

29. What do I hope to discover about myself through this journey, and how do I believe it will help me become my best self?

30. What specific behaviors, patterns, or emotional reactions do I want to understand and change through shadow work?

31. What positive changes do I hope to experience, and how do I want to feel at the end of this journey?

OVERCOMING FEARS & CHALLENGES

32. What fears, apprehensions, or concerns do I have about shadow work, and how can I address them?

33. What small steps can I take to begin my shadow work journey?

34. What strategies will I use to cope with difficult emotions or resistance that may arise?

35. How will I ensure I am compassionate and patient with myself throughout this process?

36. How will I create a safe and supportive environment for my shadow work?

TOOLS, RESOURCES & SUPPORT

37. What resources (books, mentors, tools) will I use to support my shadow work?

38. What support system (friends, family, therapist) do I have in place to help me through this journey?

39. What affirmations or mantras will I use to reinforce my commitment to this journey?

40. What daily or weekly practices will I incorporate to support my shadow work?

41. What creative, movement-based, or expressive practices can help me process and release what arises during shadow work?

42. Who or what can provide me with the support and encouragement I need for shadow work?

ACCOUNTABILITY & PROGRESS

43. Where do I feel the most safe and comfortable to engage in deep introspection?

44. How will I stay accountable and measure my progress to ensure shadow work remains a priority in my life?

45. What are my short-term goals for shadow work (e.g., within the next month)?

46. What are my long-term goals for shadow work (e.g., over the next year)?

47. What milestones and achievements will I recognize to celebrate my progress and define success in my shadow work journey?

48. How will I handle setbacks or slow progress in my shadow work?

INTEGRATION & EMBODIMENT

49. How can I integrate the insights gained from shadow work into my daily life?

50. How can I remain kind to myself, grounded, and present during intense or uncomfortable emotional experiences?

51. What practices can help me stay connected to my intentions and goals during challenging times?

52. What strengths and qualities do I possess that will support me in my shadow work?

53. How can I cultivate a mindset of growth and stay motivated throughout my shadow work journey?

54. How will I balance shadow work with other aspects of my life while staying grounded during intense emotions?

55. How can I honor and embrace the aspects of my shadow self instead of rejecting or fearing them?

EXPANSION & IMPACT

56. What lessons have I learned from past experiences that I can apply to my shadow work journey?

57. What commitments am I making to myself for this shadow work journey?

58. What daily routines or rituals can help me stay connected to my shadow work intentions?

59. How will I use the insights gained from shadow work to positively impact those around me?

PREPARATION

60. How can I use my shadow work insights to inspire and support others in their healing?

61. What does a successful shadow work journey look like to me, and how will I know when I've achieved it?

PHASE III
Illumination, Direction and Support

Before true transformation can begin, we must prepare—building a support system, gathering tools, and strengthening our foundation. This phase is about recognizing what we need, embracing guidance, and stepping into the journey with intention.

In my personal journey building the right support system took time and effort. I "kissed a few frogs" before finding the right therapist. Traditional therapy often dismissed my spiritual beliefs—sometimes with an eye roll—leaving me frustrated. But I refused to compromise my truth. My healing had to align with both my values and real-life circumstances.

My self-care routine already included yoga, nature walks, exercise, journaling and daily Tarot introspection, but I needed someone to help me integrate different perspectives. The Universe answered my call. My therapist was truly a gift from the universe, not only was she well-versed in holistic practices and Ayurveda but also deeply attuned to spiritual insights. With her, I found validation, understanding, and guidance that resonated.

Alongside my spiritual conviction, discovering my neurodivergence brought profound clarity. It dismantled years of self-doubt and released the pressure to conform. This realization activated an unshakable "Zero-F*cks-Given" energy—I no longer felt like a burden, and I refused to shrink myself for others. I no longer needed to settle for less, bend over backwards to fit in or explain myself to anyone out of feeling inadequate.

I remember thinking, "Shadow work? Of course! That explains everything." It was a new term for the inner work I had been trying to express all along.

That's when I fully embraced the depth of my being—and found the missing key. It wasn't just self-reflection; I created an intentional, fluid and deeply transformative inner work structure for myself. I had already been doing it in one way or another—a bit here, a bit there—but now I saw the urgency and the power in committing to it fully, in a concise, continuous, and strategic way as a self-devotion practice.

Scheduling therapy sessions helped me to establish consistency, but my intuition, spiritual connection, and conviction carried me through. Personal agency became my compass, guiding me to self-awareness, self-trust, and radical self-acceptance.

JOURNEY WITHIN DOORWAY #3:
The Lantern (Illumination and Awareness)

Once we accept the call, we leap —or descend— into our inner world. Here, we set our intentions, establish our why, and claim space for transformation. Spirit reminds us: the power has always been within us. You are the Magician.

In Tarot storytelling, The Magician holds all the tools needed for mastery, while The High Priestess reveals that these tools reside within. This mirrors our journey: the moment we awaken, our Lantern ignites, illuminating what was once obscured.

The Lantern represents conscious illumination—the light of self-awareness that reveals our hidden shadows. Like shining a flashlight into darkness, it dissolves the unknown, exposing what we need to address. It is both a beacon of clarity and a tool of deep introspection.

For example, in my case each therapy session, each tarot spread, each journal prompt or moment of self-reflection—these were the sparks that kept my Lantern lit.

The Lantern guides but does not dictate. It exposes, but it is up to us to engage, process, and transform. True enlightenment comes not from simply seeing our shadows, but from understanding, integrating, and reclaiming them.

It grants clarity, allowing us to navigate our inner world with purpose rather than fear. Self-awareness is key. With every step, we uncover truths, shift perspectives, and dissolve illusions.

Have you ever heard the phrase *"The Kingdom of God lives within you?"*

It speaks loudly of sovereignty—affirming, even enforcing, our innate gifts.

This metaphor reinforces the truth that divinity, wisdom, and power reside within us—not as something external we must seek or chase.

We're born with these gifts as living proof of our connection to Source and our like-God essence.

I wholeheartedly believe this saying aligns with The Lantern symbology—it represents illumination, self-awareness, and the inner light of consciousness.

Turning on the Lantern is the act of awakening... self-realizing... and, ultimately, self-actualizing. The Lantern illuminates the path—our Journey Within—which leads to recognizing our true essence, embodying our most authentic version, and fulfilling our life's purpose.

JOURNEY WITHIN DOORWAY #4:
The Compass (Direction and Alignment)

Illumination alone is not enough; we need direction. The Compass represents our internal GPS—our intuitive guide that keeps us aligned with our truth. Powered by our connection to Source and anchored in our highest self, it ensures we navigate life with intention and trust.

In times of uncertainty, the Compass grounds us in the present while keeping our vision aligned with the bigger picture. Unlike external maps with rigid paths, it is fluid and intuitive, allowing for adjustments, course corrections, and divine detours. The goal is not perfection but alignment—moving in harmony with our authentic self.

More than a directional tool, the Compass is a symbol of inner wisdom, anchoring us to our true north—our most authentic self. When we stray, it nudges us back through synchronicities, gut feelings, and moments of clarity, reminding us that we already know the way; we just need to listen.

The Compass feels like an unwavering inner pull—a deep sense of knowing that you are being guided in the right direction, even when the path ahead isn't fully clear. It's the subtle yet undeniable force that tugs at your core, urging you toward alignment.

You can experience the Compass as:

- **A gut instinct**—a quiet but firm nudge that says, this is right or this isn't for you.
- **A sense of clarity**—even in uncertainty, you just know the next step, even if it's small.

PREPARATION

- **An inner peace**—when something is aligned, tension dissolves, and you exhale in trust.
- **A magnetic pull**—a gravitational force drawing you toward what resonates.
- **A sacred whisper**—an intuitive voice reminding you, you are on the right path.

When ignored, the Compass manifests as unease, confusion, or resistance—signs of misalignment. But when honored, it becomes a steady guide, leading us forward with trust, even in the unknown.

JOURNEY WITHIN DOORWAY #5:
The Cloak (Protection and Divine Support)

When it comes to shadow work, we are never truly alone. Even in the depths of our healing journey—when the weight feels heaviest—we are safe, divinely guided, and divinely protected. The Cloak is Spirit's way of ensuring we are held and supported. It is both an external shield, guarding us from energies that do not serve us, and an internal force of resilience, strengthening us from within.

For some, the Cloak manifests as spiritual guides, ancestors, or divine presence. For others, it appears as trusted companions, soul family, or intuitive knowing. It is the energetic embrace that surrounds us when we step into the unknown.

I am very much a Hermit, and my Cloak is woven and deeply rooted in the spiritual realm. My human inner circle is small, and my biological family is almost absent. Yet, I have never felt unprotected. Spirit ensures I am covered, always.

As we dive within, The Cloak absorbs fear, softens the impact of tower moments, and reminds us that we are safe. It strengthens our foundation so we can dismantle what no longer serves us without losing ourselves in the process.

The Cloak doesn't shield us from growth—it ensures we survive it. It is not a barrier but a buffer, allowing us to embrace transformation without collapsing under its weight.

Just as a physical cloak or a (supportive and loving) mother's embrace offers warmth and comfort, this energy shields our spirit, grounding us in moments of fear and uncertainty. The knowing of this protection becomes immediate and undeniable—a sacred reminder that, even in our darkest hours, we are held by the Universe. Never alone. Always supported.

We may not always see it, but we feel it. In moments of doubt, pain, or fear, the Cloak manifests as:

- An unexpected act of kindness
- A sudden sense of peace amid chaos
- The right book, message, or person showing up at the perfect time
- The feeling of being watched over and guided

The Cloak is divine assurance. It whispers, "You are held. You are protected. You are not alone."

Moving Forward with Trust

- With the Lantern, we see.
- With the Compass, we navigate.
- With the Cloak, we are shielded.

The journey within is not linear. There will be detours, pauses, and recalibrations. But with an open mind, open heart and these innate tools, we can move forward with clarity, alignment, and unwavering trust in our own becoming.

Know Thyself: Introspections 062-064

62. The Lantern: What truths am I ready to see about myself, even if they challenge my current perception?

63. The Compass: Am I moving toward choices and relationships that align with my true desires, or am I being guided by fear or external expectations?

64. The Cloak: What boundaries or support do I need in order to feel safe and grounded as I navigate this journey?

HERO'S MILESTONE 5
Meeting the Mentors

Speaking of the importance of having the right support system—when The Fool answers the Call to Adventure and encounters the Mentor, a pivotal shift unfolds. Through this guidance, they receive wisdom, support, and the means to navigate their path. Here, the Hero awakens to their gifts, new abilities, and deeper knowledge. This phase is a profound activation of self-awareness, marking the beginning of true empowerment.

In the Hero's Journey this is what typically happens:

- **Acceptance of Change:** By answering the call, The Fool steps into the unknown, leaving behind comfort and familiarity. This marks the beginning of personal growth and transformation, acknowledging that change is both inevitable and necessary for evolution.

- **A Safe Haven for Growth:** The Mentor offers guidance but does not do the work for The Fool. Instead, they create an environment of safety and encouragement, fostering confidence and courage. The Fool must take responsibility for their journey, but with the support of a guiding presence.

- **Introduction to New Knowledge and Tools:** The Mentor provides The Fool with wisdom, skills, or tools essential for the journey ahead. Whether through direct teachings, symbolic gifts, or practical guidance, the Mentor prepares The Fool to face upcoming challenges. Often, the Mentor is someone who has traveled a similar path and offers insight to help navigate the unknown.

- **Activation of The Fool's Potential:** Meeting the Mentor often awakens dormant abilities, intuitive gifts, or deeper self-awareness. At first, The Fool may not fully grasp their capabilities, but the Mentor's presence helps activate what was previously unconscious.

- **First Test of Trust:** Trusting the Mentor can be a challenge. The Fool may be skeptical or hesitant, but taking a leap of faith is a key step in personal growth. Trusting the process, the Mentor, and their own intuition sets the stage for deeper transformation.

- **Preparation for the Road Ahead:** The Mentor equips The Fool with essential lessons, perspectives, and tools—whether physical, mental, or spiritual—so they are ready to face the trials ahead.

In short, when The Fool accepts the Call and meets the Mentor, they step into a space of growth, learning, and self-discovery. The Mentor plays a crucial role in unlocking their potential, offering wisdom and support that ensures The Fool is no longer alone but prepared for the challenges ahead.

ILLUMINATION

The Mentor in The Fool's Journey is not always a literal person.

In Tarot storytelling, the Mentor is often represented by The Magician, marking the moment when The Fool begins to uncover their power and tools. This stage signifies the Hero gaining new abilities and knowledge, embodying the message: "You have everything you need within you."

The Magician represents the integration of mind, body, and spirit, empowering The Fool to harness creative power and manifest their desires.

Another perspective on the Mentor is seen in The Hierophant, symbolizing tradition, culture, education, religion, and structured wisdom. These systems can offer foundational guidance, but they do not always facilitate self-actualization. The Hierophant represents both the benefits and limitations of external knowledge. I'll dive deeper into The Hierophant's role and challenges in the next chapter.

Yet, wisdom is not always taught—it is also remembered. Here, The High Priestess emerges as a guide to inner knowing. While The Magician and The Hierophant focus on external tools and structured learning, The High Priestess whispers: "Sometimes, the greatest wisdom comes from within." She represents intuition, the subconscious, and the mysteries that cannot be taught but must be experienced. The Fool must learn to trust their inner voice, decipher the hidden messages of dreams and symbols, and recognize that silence often holds more truth than spoken words.

At times, external mentors provide crucial structure, but true mastery requires internalization and discernment. Balancing these two types of mentorship is essential—sometimes we need a guide, and sometimes we must trust our inner wisdom to navigate the path ahead.

While many seek guidance from a teacher or coach, mentorship is not always tangible. The Universe speaks in symbols, experiences, and inner wisdom, offering guidance in unexpected forms. The Mentor can take many forms, often representing forces, tools, resources, or archetypal energies that guide The Fool through their journey.

The Mentor might manifest in different ways:

- **Inner Wisdom:** The Fool's own intuition or inner voice guiding them forward. Recognizing this guidance often requires stillness and trust—if an idea, urge, or knowing keeps surfacing, it may be your inner mentor speaking.

- **Synchronicities:** Meaningful coincidences and signs from the Universe directing the way. When patterns emerge—seeing the same symbol, hearing the same phrase, or encountering repeated themes—it's worth paying attention. These moments often confirm that you're aligned with your path.

- **Life Lessons & Challenges:** Adversity itself as a teacher, pushing The Fool to grow. Hardships often force transformation. Rather than resisting, ask: What is this moment teaching me? What new strength or skill is emerging from this?

- **Nature:** Powerful encounters with the natural world that offer wisdom and grounding. A sudden connection with an animal, the cycles of the moon, or the whispers of the wind can all serve as messengers, reminding us to attune ourselves to greater forces.

- **Spiritual Guides & Archetypes:** Ancestors, angels, deities, or unseen forces providing insight. Whether through meditation, dreams, or ritual, these mentors appear when we are ready to receive their lessons.

- **Books, Music, or Art:** A song, book, or work of art that carries a profound message. Sometimes, a single phrase or melody speaks directly to our soul, providing the wisdom we need in that moment.

- **Symbols or Dreams:** Messages revealed through dreams, visions, or subconscious insights. Keeping a journal of recurring symbols and dreams can help reveal themes that are guiding you forward.

So, how do we recognize when we are receiving mentorship from a non-traditional source? The key is awareness and trust. The Fool must learn to listen—to their intuition, to the signs around them, and to the lessons hidden in each experience.

JOURNEY WITHIN: DYNAMICS OF SHADOW WORK

How do we balance external and internal mentorship? The Magician teaches self-empowerment, while The Hierophant offers structured wisdom. One is about personal mastery, the other about inherited knowledge. Neither is absolute. When feeling lost, ask: Do I need external guidance right now, or is this a moment to trust myself? Sometimes, the greatest wisdom comes from within.

Whether external or internal, seen or unseen, the Mentor plays a vital role in The Fool's journey—offering guidance, unlocking potential, and preparing them for transformation. The Fool may not always recognize the lesson in the moment, but in hindsight, every step of the journey reveals itself as part of a greater unfolding helping The Fool rise to the next level of their path.

INNER KNOWING

- **The High Priestess —** Intuition, psychic Insight, sacred secrets, knowledge, deep awareness
- **The Hermit —** Inner light, soul-searching, truth-seeking, discernment, wisdom, self-initiation

# CHAPTER FOUR
APPLICATION

Application is the process of putting knowledge into action. It is the bridge between understanding and transformation—where concepts, insights, and theories become lived experiences. In any personal growth journey, application is what moves us from passive awareness to active engagement. Without it, knowledge remains abstract, and change remains a possibility rather than a reality.

In shadow work, application refers to *how* we engage in the process. It's about doing the work—actively confronting unconscious patterns, integrating repressed aspects of the self, and making conscious choices that align with your true nature.

Application in shadow work involves:

- **Choosing an Approach** — Selecting the methods and philosophies that best support your journey into the shadow self.

- **Unveiling & Accepting Your Shadows** — Recognizing the aspects of yourself that you have rejected, denied, or suppressed and bringing them into awareness.

- **Understanding Your Shadow Self** — Exploring its origins, patterns, and influence on your thoughts, reactions, and behaviors.

- **Exploring Your Shadow Profile** — Identifying and mapping the different ways your shadow manifests, including recurring themes, patterns, and archetypes.

- **Working with Your Shadow Self —** Engaging in practices that transform the shadow into a source of strength, creativity, and authenticity through integration, healing, and transformation.

This chapter marks the transition from preparation to action. It is an invitation to step fully into the work—to face what has been hidden, to engage in what has been avoided, and to transform what has long remained in the dark.

Now, the real work begins. And you got this!

SECTION 17: APPROACHES

There are various methods for approaching shadow work, ranging from simple daily journaling to structured, step-by-step programs. Some may choose traditional therapy or spiritual life coaching, while others explore a blend of psychological and spiritual practices. Additionally, self-care rituals—such as movement, time in nature, and balanced nourishment—can provide essential support, grounding, and integration as you navigate this inner journey.

I am keeping this section short and sweet. And to the point. Let's go over approaches together.

For a deeper dive, I invite you to explore the accompanying video inside our online blueprint, where I break down popular approaches and provide practical guidance to help you choose what resonates most. Each approach offers unique insights and tools. What works best will depend on your individual needs, preferences, and the depth of work you are ready to engage in.

Embrace this transformative path with an open heart and mind. The rewards of shadow work are profound, leading to a more authentic, self-aware, and empowered you.

E-COURSE LECTURE: "Exploring Shadow Work Approaches"

SECTION 18. UNVEILING YOUR SHADOW SELF

No matter which approaches you choose, the goal is to unveil your shadow self.

Carl Jung's concept of the **Shadow Self** is one of the most profound aspects of his analytical psychology. The **Shadow** represents the unconscious parts of ourselves that we repress, reject, or deny–often because they conflict with our ideal self-image or societal expectations. These hidden aspects include fears, desires, impulses, weaknesses, and even untapped strengths.

At its core, the Shadow is the part of the psyche the ego refuses to acknowledge. It contains everything we have disowned due to conditioning, trauma, or moral judgment. However, it is neither purely negative nor entirely destructive–it is simply unconscious and misunderstood. Still, it continues to surface in various archetypal forms:

- **The Outcast** — The rejected or misunderstood part of oneself.
- **The Trickster** — The unpredictable, chaotic aspect that disrupts illusions.
- **The Dark Twin** — The "other self" that represents what is denied.
- **The Beast** — Raw instincts, primal emotions, and unfiltered power.
- **The Hidden Gift** — Suppressed talents, potential, or wisdom waiting to emerge.

JOURNEY WITHIN: DYNAMICS OF SHADOW WORK

The Shadow Self is our subconscious—the realm where all of our shadows reside. It encompasses the hidden, denied, ignored, or repressed aspects of our psyche.

The Shadow isn't just personal—it exists beyond archetypes on a collective level as well. Societies, cultures, and even family systems have collective shadows that dictate unspoken rules, biases, and behaviors. The more we understand our personal shadow, the better equipped we are to navigate the world consciously, breaking free from inherited patterns and limitations.

In our masterclass, **"Shadow Self: The Sacred Unknown"** we expand on shadow profiles, narratives, and themes, exploring what unfolds when we embark on the journey within—or when we avoid it entirely.

We examine the key distinction between:

- **Working with Your Shadow Self** — Identifying your shadow profile, recognizing personal narratives, and learning how to address shadow themes.

- **Walking in Your Shadow Self** — Understanding the consequences of avoidance and exploring what it means to become or embody a dark archetype.

This passage—and the entire foundation of this book—is about the first path: **working on your shadow self** by embarking on the Journey Within and doing the work. But let's clarify this important notion: We do shadow work to unveil our shadows and reveal the shadow self ready for healing and growth.

APPLICATION

You engage with your hidden aspects consciously, intentionally, and with a willingness to heal and integrate. Walking as your shadow self, on the other hand, means being ruled by unhealed wounds, suppressed emotions, and unconscious patterns without self-awareness or accountability.

Working With Your Shadow Self (Empowered)

- Acknowledging, exploring, and understanding suppressed emotions.
- Facing your triggers with curiosity, not defensiveness.
- Taking responsibility for your healing and personal growth.
- Recognizing that your shadow is a part of you, but not all of you.
- Integrating lessons from past wounds to step into self-mastery.

This path leads to: Growth, healing, wholeness, emotional intelligence, and deep self-acceptance.

Walking As Your Shadow Self (Disempowered)

- Unconsciously projecting unresolved wounds onto others.
- Allowing fears, doubts, or negative beliefs to control your decisions.

- Identifying with your trauma instead of working through it.
- Embodying or justifying toxic patterns rather than healing them.
- Resisting self-awareness and remaining stuck in cycles of pain.

This path leads to: Stagnation, self-sabotage, repeating toxic cycles, and emotional distress.

E-COURSE LECTURE: "Identifying Shadows"

Know Thyself: Introspections 065-071

THE SHADOW SELF

65. Root Chakra: What fears or insecurities prevent me from feeling grounded and safe?

66. Sacral Chakra: Where have I suppressed my emotions, desires, or creativity out of fear?

67. Solar Plexus Chakra: What limiting beliefs about my power and confidence hold me back?

68. Heart Chakra: What past wounds or resentments block me from giving or receiving love?

69. Throat Chakra: Where in my life am I silencing my truth, and what fears are behind it?

70. Third Eye Chakra: What illusions or mental patterns cloud my ability to see clearly?

71. Crown Chakra: What attachments or ego-driven thoughts keep me disconnected from divine flow?

SECTION 19. UNDERSTANDING AND ACCEPTING THE SHADOW SELF

One of the biggest myths about shadow work is that it's dangerous—that working with your shadow self is something to fear. But let's dismantle that right now. Shadow work is not dangerous, and your shadow self is not out to get you. On the contrary, this process is empowering, liberating, and deeply transformative.

What feeds this myth is not the shadow itself, but the vulnerability that comes with facing it. When we unveil our shadows, we expose parts of ourselves that may have been buried, misunderstood, or rejected. If we don't understand or accept them, they can feel overwhelming. But this is where significance, openness, readiness, intention, and choosing the right approach make all the difference.

The shadow self is simply where our shadows reside—the hidden, denied, ignored, or repressed aspects of our psyche. In Jungian psychology, the Shadow represents unconscious parts of ourselves that are not readily accessible to our conscious awareness. This concept is integral to Carl Jung's archetypes: the persona, the shadow, the anima/animus, and the self.

Our shadow self plays a significant role in self-mastery and individuation. Engaging in shadow work—unveiling and addressing these hidden aspects—promotes balance, wholeness, and personal growth. However, ignoring or rationalizing these shadows can lead to "walking as the shadow self," where unresolved traits and wounds dominate one's identity and behavior.

APPLICATION

Understanding and accepting your shadow self is both an internal shift and an external transformation. It's not just a conceptual process—it's something you feel in your body, mind, and spirit. It's the difference between fighting yourself and embracing yourself fully.

Shadow work isn't about suffering—it's about liberation. It's a journey of progression, not perfection. I've been doing my own shadow work -ongoing- for years now and to give you an insider's perspective, here's what understanding and accepting your shadow self looks like and feels like in practice:

The Feels:

- At first, it may feel raw, vulnerable, and even uncomfortable. You are facing parts of yourself that were once hidden or repressed.

- Then, it feels clarifying and liberating. You see patterns for what they are and realize you have the power to change them. You're becoming more self-aware, intuitive, and at peace with yourself.

- Next, it feels empowering. You make choices with awareness, confidence, and self-trust—rather than reacting from unconscious wounds.

- Finally, it feels whole, peaceful, and aligned. You no longer fear yourself—you embrace all of you. You experience a deep sense of wholeness, feeling aligned, connected, and at home within yourself.

The Unfolding: As you get to meet your shadow self and you work on your wounds a new and stronger you start unfolding! This is part of the healing process:

- **Acknowledging and Naming Your Hidden Aspects:** Before you can work with your shadow, you must recognize it. You start to see suppressed emotions, fears, and patterns that have been shaping your thoughts and behaviors. You start noticing the why behind your behaviors instead of pretending they don't exist.

- **Recognizing Your Triggers Without Reacting Defensively:** Triggers become teachers instead of enemies. You notice what upsets you, but instead of lashing out or shutting down, you reflect on why it affects you. Instead of immediately blaming others or shutting down when triggered, you pause, reflect, and ask, "Where is this coming from? What is this teaching me?"

- **No Longer Running from Your Emotions:** You stop suppressing, avoiding, or numbing your feelings. Instead of distractions and unhealthy coping mechanisms, you allow yourself to process emotions fully. You allow yourself to fully feel rather than ignore or seek distractions, overworking, or unhealthy habits.

- **Seeing Your Flaws Without Shame:** Imperfection is not a flaw—it's part of your humanity. You stop self-punishing and meet yourself with compassion instead of judgment. You don't beat yourself up for past mistakes, negative thoughts, or insecurities. Instead, you meet yourself with self-compassion and self-acceptance.

APPLICATION

- **Taking Responsibility for Your Healing:** You step out of victimhood and reclaim your power. Instead of waiting for external validation or change, you take ownership of your transformation. You actively seek tools, support, and practices that help you grow.

- **Releasing Old Stories and Outdated Identities:** Your past does not define you. You release limiting beliefs, trauma narratives, and labels that no longer serve your highest good. You stop defining yourself by past wounds, failures, or external labels. You accept your role as the creator of your life.

- **Speaking Your Truth Without Fear of Rejection:** You no longer shrink yourself to be accepted. You express your needs, boundaries, and truth with clarity and confidence – no room for guilt or fear. You no longer dim your light or hide parts of yourself to accommodate others.

- **Developing Greater Self-Awareness and Intuition:** Your inner guidance strengthens. You recognize patterns before they take control and make intentional choices rather than unconscious reactions.

- **Feeling Less Triggered by Others:** Other people's actions no longer dictate your peace. You stop personalizing everything and gain emotional sovereignty over your reactions.

- **Experiencing a Deep Sense of Wholeness:** At last, you integrate and embrace every part of yourself. There is no more inner battle–just self-alignment, empowerment, and peace.

In essence, understanding and accepting your shadow self means no longer fearing your own reflection. There is no boogeyman—only a part of you seeking understanding and healing. It's about looking into the depths of your being with love, curiosity, and courage, and realizing that every aspect of you is worthy of integration, healing, and empowerment.

APPLICATION

SECTION 20. OUR SHADOW PROFILE

Our shadow profile is the structured representation of an individual's shadow self—a unique outline or "map of the cave." This profile reflects personal subconscious patterns, unhealed wounds, and unresolved emotions. Like fingerprints, each person's shadow profile is distinct.

This is the collection of your shadows and how they manifest: aspects, themes, narratives, etc.

- Shadow profiles are patterns, traits, and behaviors that stem from unresolved wounds, fears, conditioning, and suppressed aspects of the self.
- These profiles are not who we are at our core, but they shape how we show up in the world when we operate from unhealed wounds.

It's All Vibrational

One of the greatest benefits of shadow work is how it improves our manifestation power. Understanding the vibrational impact of your shadow profile is crucial for reclaiming energetic sovereignty.

Your shadow profile shapes your energetic frequency because every thought, belief, and emotion carries a vibrational signature.

When your shadow profile operates unconsciously, it keeps you locked in lower vibrational states—fear, guilt, shame, resentment, or self-doubt. These emotions become habitual frequencies, reinforcing the very patterns that created them in the first place.

Your shadow profile also influences how you react to experiences, which in turn reinforces your vibrational state. If left unchecked, these repeated reactions become your predominant energetic pattern, shaping the way you engage with yourself, others, and the world.

Your shadow profile isn't just a psychological construct—it dictates the frequency you hold. The frequency you hold determines the reality you attract. If you are going to memorize and anchor anything form this book, let it be this: **Your shadow profile directly influences your predominant vibrational state, which in turn affects what you attract and manifest in your reality.**

Our predominant vibrational state (PVS) represents the overall frequency at which our thoughts, emotions, and energy resonate most of the time. This vibration dictates how our energy flows and influences our manifestations. Addressing our shadow self is crucial for raising and maintaining a high PVS, enabling us to live more authentic, fulfilling and authentic lives.

The Shadow-Magnetism Connection

Manifestation isn't just about conscious desires—it's also about subconscious energy. If your shadow profile operates unconsciously, it holds unresolved fears, doubts, and limiting beliefs that emit low-frequency vibrations (scarcity, unworthiness, rejection). These vibrations signal the universe and shape the circumstances, relationships, and experiences you unconsciously call in.

For example:

- If your shadow profile is rooted in abandonment wounds, you may unknowingly manifest relationships that reinforce rejection or emotional unavailability.
- If your shadow profile carries deep-seated scarcity beliefs, you may find yourself attracting financial struggles despite actively trying to create abundance.

From both personal experience and my work as a shadow work coach, I've identified three key aspects of the shadow self—or forces in motion—which I call the Shadow Profile Snapshot:

- **Energy** (Spiritual/Vibrational)
- **Emotion** (Emotional)
- **Mindset** (Mental)

These three forces—energy, emotion, and mindset—do not operate in isolation. They weave together, reinforcing patterns that shape our lived experience. For example, an abandonment-based shadow can manifest across energy, mindset, and emotional aspects in distinct yet interconnected ways:

- **Emotion:** Avoiding intimacy, fearing closeness and vulnerability, and rejecting deep connections to prevent potential abandonment.

- **Energy:** Becoming clingy or hypervigilant—unconsciously seeking attachment, comfort, and validation to fill an inner void left by abandonment—leading to imbalanced relationships.
- **Mindset:** Developing an anxious attachment style, constantly worrying about the stability of relationships and the intentions of others.

Now, let me give you a different scenario involving a complex, layered wound: abandonment triggering betrayal—or vice versa.

Abandonment and betrayal wounds often trigger each other, but the sequence may vary based on someone's life experience, attachment style, and nervous system imprinting.

Here's how they intertwine:

- Someone with an abandonment wound, fearing dismissal or being left behind, may become hypervigilant to signs of disloyalty or deception—fueling a betrayal wound.
- Someone who has been lied to, cheated on, or emotionally deceived may internalize that betrayal as proof they are unworthy of love, safety, or loyalty—deepening the abandonment wound.

In essence:
Abandonment says: "You left me because I'm not enough."
Betrayal says: "You hurt me when I trusted you."
But both wounds point to a core fear: "I am not safe in connection."

When these wounds remain unhealed, they emit a vibration of distrust and the expectation of betrayal, manifesting as:

- Calling in relationships that reinforce the betrayal pattern.
- Self-sabotaging connections by acting out of fear rather than trust.
- · Blocking manifestations of abundance, support, and love due to subconscious resistance: "I don't want to be let down again."

This is how it may manifest across the Shadow Profile Snapshot:

- **Emotional Manifestation (Emotional Body)**
  - Chronic distrust in relationships, even when there's no evidence of betrayal.
  - Fear of being vulnerable or open with others, leading to emotional walls.
  - Resentment and difficulty forgiving—even long after the betrayal occurred.
  - A tendency to test people's loyalty, sometimes unconsciously pushing them away.

- **Energy Manifestation (Spiritual/Vibrational Body)**
  - Holding onto past betrayals like energetic scars, creating a subconscious expectation of future betrayals.

- Attracting relationships that mirror unresolved betrayal themes (e.g., dishonest partners or deceptive friendships).
- Oscillating between hyper-independence ("I don't need anyone") and deep loneliness: "Why does no one show up for me?"

- **Mindset Manifestation (Mental Body)**
  - Developing limiting beliefs such as "People always disappoint me" or "I can't trust anyone."
  - Overanalyzing others' actions, assuming hidden motives or deception.
  - Struggling to accept genuine kindness without suspicion.
  - Internalizing betrayal as proof of unworthiness: "If they betrayed me, I must not be enough."

The Role of Shadow Narratives

Our shadow self generates what we refer to as **Shadow Narratives**—the subconscious stories we tell ourselves based on past wounds, fears, and conditioning. These narratives silently influence our thoughts, emotions, and energetic frequency—often without conscious awareness.

Shadow narratives don't just affect how we relate to others; they also shape our self-perception, decision-making, and the energetic signals we emit—and therefore, what we manifest.

APPLICATION

For instance:

- Someone with a betrayal wound may adopt a scarcity mindset in relationships, believing love must be earned or tightly controlled to avoid loss.
- They may unconsciously attract emotionally unavailable partners, reinforcing the belief that trust is dangerous.
- Alternatively, they might become hyper-independent, avoiding deep connections to prevent potential betrayal.

How to Address Shadow Narratives

We have the power to shift the narrative by consciously choosing to reframe and reclaim.

In this scenario—abandonment and betrayal—healing the betrayal wound begins with reclaiming trust, not in others first, but within yourself. Healing the abandonment wound, on the other hand, begins with choosing yourself consistently—showing up for your needs, validating your worth, and no longer abandoning yourself in pursuit of connection.

Recognize that trust begins within.

The shift from "I can't trust others" to "I trust myself to navigate relationships with wisdom" is a powerful reframe that restores sovereignty over your energy and manifestations.

Common betrayal and/or abandonment wound narratives include:

- "People always leave."
- "I must protect myself at all costs."
- "Trusting others only leads to disappointment."

These beliefs reinforce distrust, shaping behavior, energy, and ultimately, the reality you manifest. When left unexamined, they create cycles of self-sabotage—pushing people away or attracting situations that validate the fear of betrayal.

The key to rewriting these narratives is awareness and choice.

When you identify the unconscious beliefs driving your patterns, you regain the power to shift them. When you shift your inner narrative, your external reality follows.

The energy you embody dictates the experiences you manifest.

SECTION 21: WORKING WITH THE SHADOW SELF

Working with your shadow self means engaging in practices that transform hidden wounds into sources of strength, creativity, power, and authenticity through integration, healing, and transformation. True healing begins with the right energy, guidance, tools, and approach.

Healing and integrating your shadow self raises your vibration and aligns you with your authentic essence, improving not just your manifestation process but also your ability to co-create and/or influence your highest reality.

We all carry wounds and imbalances shaped by our lived experiences. Life's natural fragility makes us vulnerable, and after events like a global crisis, many of us are left with shattered or scattered energetic fields—blocked, leaking, or disconnected from our life force. In survival mode, we may unconsciously attach ourselves to people, places, objects, or circumstances that once provided comfort, stability, or security in uncertain times.

However, when we remain tethered to what has already served its purpose—whether a relationship, mindset, environment, or belief—it can shift from a source of support to a source of stagnation. What once felt safe may become toxic, counterproductive, or a full-fledged energetic blockage. These unresolved attachments create resistance, challenges, and energetic cords in need of severing.

Doing the Work

As individuals and as a collective, we experience imbalances through the ups and downs of life. The depth and intensity of these imbalances depend on how we process them. Any encounter with fear, pain, chaos, trauma, breakups, disappointment, stress, or shock leaves imprints on our physical, mental, emotional, spiritual, and energetic bodies. When left unaddressed, these wounds compromise our vessel, making us susceptible to dysfunction and disconnection.

Over time, unresolved energies accumulate in our chakras, auric field, and energetic layers, burdening us with negativity, anxiety, guilt, shame, grief, sadness, anger, oppression, and distorted perceptions of reality. This fragmentation causes us to lose our sense of self, making us question our trust, faith, safety, purpose, potential, and ability to move forward.

Shadow work—working with your shadow self—is an invitation to explore your innermost layers, to identify, dissect, transmute, and release all that is stagnant, toxic, fragmented, or outdated. Whether these wounds stem from karmic cycles, ancestral lineage, past lives, childhood, or recent experiences, they can obstruct your emotional, spiritual, mental, physical, social, and financial well-being.

Shadow work is an intimate, transformative journey—one that requires the right approach, tools, and environment to ensure deep, lasting healing. It's not just about confronting your wounds; it's about creating a space where you can process, release, and reclaim yourself fully.

Yes, the journey inward is yours to walk, but how you navigate it makes all the difference. Shadow work is deep, raw, and complex—it unearths buried emotions, subconscious patterns, and painful truths. Without structure, a guiding framework, or a supportive presence, it's easy to become overwhelmed, stuck, or confused.

For this reason, I always recommend having some level of structure and support when doing shadow work. Not because you need someone to hold your hand, but because a well-guided process keeps you from getting lost in emotional loops, stagnation, or avoidance.

- No, you don't have to break the bank or compromise your financial stability in the process.
- No, you don't have to reinvent the wheel—there are books, tools, resources, teachers, coaches, and communities available to explore.
- No, you don't need someone to "babysit" your process, but guidance and accountability can be powerful allies on this journey.

The key is finding what feels validating, keeps you inspired, and holds you accountable—without anyone doing the work for you. A structured framework, like the **One Vessel** program, is designed to provide tools, insights, and resources that support your journey in a way that honors your individuality and the sacredness of this process. It helps you:

- Stay focused on what needs to be addressed, rather than getting lost in emotional overwhelm.
- Navigate discomfort with inspiration, so fear or resistance doesn't stall your progress.

- Move through your healing with clarity, purpose, and intentional guidance.

Without the right support, shadow work can become disorienting and destabilizing. Unprocessed emotions may resurface without resolution, triggering anxiety, doubt, or emotional shutdown. Confronting your wounds alone, without a safe structure, can lead to cycles of avoidance, self-sabotage, or reinforcing limiting beliefs rather than breaking them.

But this isn't meant to make you fear shadow work–only to offer a realistic perspective. The process itself is not something to be afraid of; in fact, it is one of the most liberating and empowering journeys you can take. Having the right tools, guidance, and environment simply ensures that your healing is intentional, supported, and sustainable. Shadow work is not just about uncovering what's hidden; it's about integrating, healing, and transforming what you find. With the right approach, you don't just face your shadows—you reclaim your power from them.

Anchoring Your Healing

For those looking to begin with a guided approach, a Jumpstart Shadow Discovery Kit like *Know Thyself* – which you are already participating in- or a self-assessment tool such as Sanctuary, our conscious detachment ritual, can provide a structured and sacred space for this work. Whether performed alone, with our Majesty Candle, or our grounding jewelry as an energetic anchor, these tools allow you to navigate your shadows with intention rather than in isolation. Here, you are not left to process your wounds alone—you are held, witnessed, and empowered as you sever toxic ties and liberate yourself from what no longer serves your highest good.

In my work, I support individuals in releasing:

- People and relationships that deplete them.
- Chaotic situations that drain their energy.
- Unhealthy patterns, bad habits, and self-limiting beliefs.
- Stagnant circumstances, dead-end jobs, and negatively charged environments.
- Lingering spells, taboos, old paradigms, karmic bonds, and past-life attachments.
- Former versions of themselves that no longer align with their evolution.
- Pain from trauma, abuse, neglect, and betrayal.

Through this process, you experience firsthand what it's like to engage in shadow work in a supported environment—one where healing is not just about letting go but about intentionally rewriting your story. My role is to hold space as an alchemist, strategist, and guide, helping you move through the discomfort and into a state of self-mastery.

You are not here by accident. There is a reason you are reading this book, and there is a reason I was placed on your path. The question is not whether you are ready—the question is whether you will answer the call to reclaim yourself fully.

ILLUMINATION
Key Terminology

SHADOW: The hidden, ignored, denied, or repressed parts of the psyche. The shadow often manifests as triggers, patterns, and projections, which I refer to as soul whispers or signs—subtle yet powerful messages from our higher self, signaling that something within us needs attention.

SHADOW SELF: The subconscious realm where all our shadows reside. It is the dark cave within us, holding the aspects we have suppressed, avoided, or rejected. Exploring the shadow self is like venturing into the depths of our unconscious mind, where transformation begins.

SHADOW PROFILE: A structured representation of an individual's shadow self—a unique outline or "map of the cave." This profile reflects personal subconscious patterns, unhealed wounds, and unresolved emotions. Like fingerprints, each person's shadow profile is distinct.

SHADOW ASPECTS: The different angles or perspectives of the shadow within our psyche. In my shadow work coaching practice, I focus on three primary perspectives:

- Energy (how the shadow affects our spiritual and energetic state)

- Emotion (how it influences our feelings and responses)
- Mindset (how it shapes our beliefs, thoughts, and perceptions)

SHADOW NARRATIVE: The stories, conditioning, and beliefs we have built around our shadows. These narratives shape how we perceive ourselves, others, and the world—often reinforcing patterns of limitation, fear, or self-doubt.

SHADOW THEME: A set or template of patterns, triggers, projections, and behaviors that reveal how the shadow manifests in our lives. These themes often appear repeatedly, offering us opportunities to recognize, understand, and heal unresolved wounds.

SHADOW WORK: The inner work—the act of addressing, integrating, and transforming our shadow self. Simply put, it's "working with our shadow self" actively acknowledging and engaging with our hidden aspects instead of rejecting them. When we listen to our soul whispers—our triggers, patterns, and projections—we begin to illuminate what was once hidden. Shadow work is about turning on the flashlight: bringing awareness to our darkness, addressing our inner wounds, and embracing wholeness.

Know Thyself: Introspections 072-074

72. Energy (Spiritual/Vibrational): Where in my life do I feel the most resistance or stagnation, and what might this reveal about my alignment with my higher self?

73. Emotion (Emotional): Which emotions do I tend to suppress or overexpress, and how do these patterns shape my relationships and self-perception?

74. Mindset (Mental): What recurring thought or self-limiting belief keeps me in a cycle of fear, doubt, or self-sabotage, and how can I begin to shift it toward empowerment?

PHASE IV
Facing Your Shadows

> **JOURNEY WITHIN DOORWAY #6:**
> **The Grotto (Where Shadows and Light Collide)**

Deep within our inner landscape lies the Grotto—the sacred heart of our soul, where only love matters. It is an inner temple and initiation chamber where we confront our deepest truths. Here, the light of our Lantern illuminates even the most hidden corners, guiding us through chaos, distortion, and the wounds that have shaped us. It is within the Grotto that our Inner Magician tools become enchanted keys for transformation.

Entering the Grotto is never a light decision. Sometimes, it is a divine invitation—a gentle pull toward expansion. Other times, it is an unavoidable summons—a moment when your soul craves evolution and no longer allows avoidance. This sacred space holds room for both your shadows and your light, neither judging nor condemning—only observing. Here, your defenses fall. In the silence, you are left with nothing but the raw truth of your emotional, energetic, and mental patterns.

Shadow work was my own reluctant invitation into the Grotto. I thought I understood self-love—I was doing the work, wasn't I? But the deeper I went, the more I realized:

- I wasn't truly allowing myself to feel.
- I wasn't giving myself permission to cry, to be vulnerable, to crack open.
- I wasn't really showing up for myself.

"What?! Of course, I love myself," I told myself over and over. But it wasn't real. I had built walls so high that even I couldn't see over them.

Despite professional success, I felt unfulfilled. I was constantly "in and out of the closet," hiding parts of myself, struggling with trust issues, and reinforcing emotional barriers. It was messy. And yet, as I stepped deeper into my shadows, I began to see the toxic patterns that had kept me disconnected from my authentic self.

Alchemy in the Dark

The Grotto is where the alchemy process begins—the dismantling of the past to prepare for renewal. It is the birthplace of your light, the spark that will eventually purify and disintegrate the Phoenix, allowing it to rise from the ashes.

Initially, when I added therapy as part of my self-care, I naively expected decades of pain to dissolve within a few sessions. Vulnerability felt unnatural—almost wrong—but I committed to showing up for myself. With each step, I dove deeper into my shadows, peeling back layers I didn't even realize existed.

As a double water sign, emotions should have been my strength, but I had suppressed them for so long that

APPLICATION

reconnecting with them felt foreign. Breaking through that emotional dam was slow. The first tears brought relief—but they weren't the end. There were deeper layers still waiting to be uncovered.

In our Journey Within, the Grotto holds our Innermost Sanctum—a sacred space where we confront shadows and tend to deep wounds, both expected and unexpected. It is a metaphorical container that serves as the locus of profound self-reflection, shadow work, healing, intentional alchemy, and inner transformation.

The Grotto is not just where we meet our pain—it is also where we encounter our infinite potential for transformation. The discomfort we feel here is not punishment but a necessary breaking open. This breaking allows light to flood into our darkness, illuminating areas of denial, repression, or resistance.

My Grotto felt raw and unfamiliar. I needed reinforcement! Tarot became my enchanted Lantern and master key, offering a structured framework to decode my personal milestones. Each card became a mirror, reflecting back the parts of myself I had struggled to see. Tarot and journaling became my self-devotion tools, helping me reclaim my personal agency, deepen my trust in my intuition, and develop the assertiveness I had long suppressed.

Not only did I survive the Grotto, but I thrived in it.

I immersed myself in every possible modality—Tarot, astrology, crystal healing, personality profiles, human design, shadow archetypes—each one unveiling new pieces of my inner puzzle. I studied the energies that shaped me, tracing the patterns that had once held me captive. This process wasn't just about understanding myself; it was about integrating every fractured piece of my being.

I will not tell you that stepping into the Grotto is easy. It is not. But I will tell you this—on the other side, you will not be the same.

The Grotto isn't just a place—it's a calling. A space that transcends physical location, existing as a state of being where trust in the process allows you to embrace discomfort, explore your depths, and honor the lessons hidden within.

Will you step inside?

HERO'S MILESTONE 6
Crossing the Threshold

In the Hero's Journey, "Crossing the Threshold" encapsulates the essence of both Sanctuary and Grotto energy. This is the Fool accepting the call and stepping into the unknown, facing fears, and embracing change and new experiences. While still unaware of their shadow, the Fool begins to venture into unfamiliar territory, preparing to confront hidden aspects of themselves.

The High Priestess stands as the Threshold Guardian, symbolizing intuition, mystery, and inner wisdom. While the Magician, as a mentor, may have provided tools, it is the High Priestess who reveals where to find them and how to use them. She appears when the Hero must rely on their instincts or delve into hidden knowledge to progress.

With the guidance of the High Priestess, the Fool begins uncovering hidden truths, intuition, and subconscious patterns. The journey shifts inward, focusing on self-discovery. This stage marks the first steps in recognizing the false self, unacknowledged fears, insecurities, emotional wounds, and the ego they have used as armor.

From the Fool's Journey perspective, the High Priestess is the second major arcana card encountered, representing the threshold between the external world and the inner realms.

She teaches the Fool:

- **Patience and Stillness:** Unlike the Magician's active energy, the High Priestess embodies passivity, urging the Fool to pause and listen.
- **Inner Knowing:** She symbolizes untapped inner knowledge, emphasizing the importance of dreams, symbols, and the subconscious mind.
- **Balance of Dualities:** Positioned between two pillars of opposites (light/dark, conscious/subconscious), the High Priestess reminds the Fool of the harmony found in duality.

This phase is a time of self-reflection, trusting one's inner compass, and learning to navigate unseen forces guiding the journey.

From the Hero's Journey perspective, the High Priestess manifests as both a gateway into the unknown and a guide or internal mentor encountered during the "Call to Adventure" or "Crossing the Threshold." She is not always a literal figure but often appears as a profound, intuitive sense, urging the Hero to trust their inner voice as they step into uncharted territory.

In real life, trusting our intuition and inner voice can feel nearly impossible when we're in the midst of our own chaos. The pain becomes overwhelming, and self-doubt creeps in. Our inner voice isn't always our most reliable guide; it's often tangled with the ego, internalized beliefs, and the inner critic, making it difficult to discern genuine inner guidance from fear-based thoughts.

Crossing my own Threshold required an immense leap of faith into the unknown: embracing vulnerability, self-love, and genuine heart-to-heart connections. It also

APPLICATION

demanded leaving behind the comfort of what was familiar: self-loathing, toxicity, and a false sense of identity that no longer served me.

My journey through shadow work wasn't just about healing old wounds; it was about unraveling how my past, societal conditioning, generational trauma, and inherited karma had shaped my beliefs, thought patterns, and actions. The walls I had built around my heart once served to protect me—but over time, they became barriers to love, healing, and transformation. It was time for them to come down.

I chose to show up for myself every single day, no matter how uncomfortable it was. That consistent commitment to my healing journey became the foundation for the deep, authentic self-love I had always craved.

I continued this process, I noticed the emerging patterns in my behavior, thoughts, and emotions, becoming increasingly aware of how much of my life had been shaped by these hidden shadows. The more I uncovered, the clearer it became: my shadows were not just pieces of pain or trauma to be discarded, but integral aspects of my journey. They held lessons, gifts, and energy that had been misplaced or misunderstood.

The more I sat with myself, the more I recognized that my shadows weren't just a collection of flaws or weaknesses; they were the areas in which I could grow the most. They were a reflection of the parts of me that needed love, acknowledgment, and healing. The shadows held the keys to my transformation, and as I embraced them, I was able to shed the armor I had built around myself. In doing so, I began to experience greater self-compassion, deeper emotional connection, and an authentic sense of wholeness.

THE ROAD OF TRIALS
Testing the Strength of My Shadows

In the Hero's Journey, The Road of Trials (somewhere between 'Crossing the Threshold' and 'Facing Tests, Allies, and Enemies') represents the Hero's tests, obstacles, and the lessons learned through struggle. For me, this phase was embodied in my persistent struggles with self-acceptance and the work required to overcome them.

My own Road of Trials was nothing short of an endeavor. Every aspect of myself that I secretly loathed was deeply rooted in the energy of The Hierophant, shaped by the weight of tradition, culture, and religion.

No, let's reframe that! Everything I hated about myself was rooted in my parents' experience of The Hierophant energy, shaped by tradition, culture, and religion. Their interpretation and embodiment of these values became the foundation of my internal struggles and the seed of deep self-hatred.

In Tarot, The Hierophant is the fifth card in the Major Arcana, symbolizing tradition, spiritual authority, and structured knowledge. It represents archetypes of guidance, communal values, and societal norms that shape beliefs—often acting as both a source of inspiration and oppression. This duality makes it a double-edged sword.

I was born and raised in a strict religious household steeped in a deeply rooted Latino, macho-patriarchal culture. Women were expected to belong to their husbands, raise children, and obey without question. Infidelity and abuse were excused under the guise of "men will be men," while the fear of God's punishment and the glorification of poverty as a gateway to heaven were impenetrable forces.

Spirituality outside of prayer or Sunday mass was condemned as rebellion against God, punishable by eternal damnation. Same-sex attraction was deemed proof of allegiance to the Devil, further reinforcing walls of judgment, discrimination, and fear.

I internalized this socio-cultural conditioning as evidence that something was deeply wrong with me. I came to believe that I was cursed, perhaps even Devil-like, damned by my existence. These beliefs, shaped by the rigid and misaligned structure of The Hierophant energy, bound me with chains of shame, guilt, and distorted perceptions of self-love, relationships, prosperity, and self-worth.

This reflection highlights the darker aspects of The Hierophant's energy when tradition and authority suppress individuality and silence the soul's truth. It was through this lens that aspects of my shadow work began—a journey to unlearn inherited wounds, dismantle distorted narratives, and reclaim my authenticity.

In the Fool's Journey, The Hierophant (Tradition) appears alongside The Empress (Mother) and The Emperor (Father) to provide authority, structure, and discipline to establish order and guidance.

However, in its misaligned state, The Hierophant often overwrites the wisdom of The High Priestess, replacing her call to inner trust and intuition with external dogma. Meaning, in its shadow form, The Hierophant often embodies the stifling of self-expression and authentic connection to one's own spiritual wisdom, instead prioritizing adherence to doctrine or authority. The role of tradition can be empowering or oppressive—whether seen as the key to unlocking our highest potential or the very source of limitations.

As I faced my shadows, I came to realize that the Road of Trials was not simply about overcoming obstacles; it was about confronting the deep emotional wounds formed by oppressive traditions.

I can affirm that much of my self-hatred and its resulting shadows, wounds, and limiting narratives of guilt and shame were deeply rooted in The Hierophant energy—manifesting through religious, cultural, familial, or societal systems that dictated what was "right," "wrong," or "worthy."

Through my shadow work, I started to regain control of my personal narrative and move towards greater self-love, acceptance, and liberation.

ILLUMINATION

The Hierophant, when distorted or corrupted, masquerades as wisdom while enforcing control. It appears as an external authority—dictating truth, demanding obedience, and severing the connection between self and divinity.

The Adversarial Hierophant: A False Authority

When misaligned, The Hierophant becomes an imposter to The High Priestess, mimicking her wisdom but offering a hollow, externalized version of spiritual truth. This masquerade reinforces dogma, control, and validation from external authorities, leading to cycles of self-doubt and shame.

It often takes the form of individuals or institutions that appear to offer guidance but instead impose restrictions, foster dependence, and mislead. We've all encountered this misaligned Hierophant energy—it's the parent who demands unquestioning obedience, the spiritual teacher who enforces rigid doctrines, the societal norms that tell us who we 'should' be. It shows up in:

- Deeply ingrained beliefs about worthiness, success, or identity shaped by cultural or familial expectations.
- Rigid adherence to outdated traditions or beliefs, demanding blind conformity without questioning authority.

- Gatekeeping in spiritual communities, reducing spirituality to rigid practices or doctrines that dismiss individual intuition and fluid self-discovery.
- Systems, people, or organizations exerting control through obedience, silence, or suppression—particularly of emotions, identity, or desires.
- Demands for external validation from hierarchical structures, institutions, or "experts," enforcing separation between the divine and the self.

The misaligned Hierophant wields fear as a tool to maintain control, discouraging introspection and exploration beyond the confines of what is deemed "acceptable."

Transformation: From Oppressor to Ally

Yet, The Hierophant energy is not inherently negative. When integrated intentionally, it becomes a powerful ally for wisdom, structure, and spiritual growth. By confronting and transforming its oppressive aspects, we can release guilt and shame, dismantle self-hatred, and reclaim the path of self-love and authenticity.

Healing the Hierophant energy involves exploring the origins of our belief systems and examining how inherited traditions, societal expectations, or learned behaviors may still shape our life.

For The Hero, challenging the Hierophant brings an opportunity to honor what aligns with their truth while releasing what no longer serves their growth. The Hero steps onto **The Chariot**, determined to seek their own

APPLICATION

truth and confront the oppressive influence of misaligned Hierophant energy. This pivotal moment symbolizes the Hero's reclamation of autonomy, balancing willpower and emotional mastery to challenge the rigid systems, traditions, and dogmas that have stifled authenticity.

Ultimately, The Chariot reminds us that while external forces may influence our journey, our inner world—our mindset, willpower, and level of self-awareness—is the key to triumph.

HONORING YOUR PROGRESS

Hey darling, you're doing amazing.

I just wanted to check in—to validate your journey and remind you that you are not alone. If at any point you find yourself craving deeper insight or guidance, know that you're supported. My contact information is included in my bio at the end of this book, along with a special invite. Feel welcome to connect with me if it resonates with you—it would be my pleasure to continue supporting you.

Let's take a moment to acknowledge how proud of yourself you should feel right now. You've shown up, invested in yourself, committed to your growth, and taken the time to deepen your understanding of shadow work. That's no small thing.

Like we've shared before: you are taking space, holding space, creating space, and occupying it. And you deserve it.

Quick question… Have you figured out your preferred shadow work approach or supportive tool yet?

Maybe you're drawn to deep introspection, expressive journaling, or meditative reflection. Perhaps it's through movement, conversation, or ritual. Whatever path feels right, trust that your process is unfolding exactly as it should.

And if you're still exploring—don't worry. There's no rush. **The truth is, you've already begun.** By picking up this book, journaling your way through the *Know Thyself* questions, and engaging with its online blueprint, you've set your self-discovery process into motion—and even jumpstarted your very own Journey Within.

Your next step isn't about how to start your shadow work—it's about how to continue cultivating. Give yourself time. Keep exploring. Stay curious about yourself.

A Sacred Tool for Self-Discovery

If you've been reading along, you might have picked up on my deep connection to Tarot—my sacred tool for self-devotion. Tarot and journaling have deepened my understanding of personal agency, sharpened my intuition, and strengthened my assertiveness. These practices have been my companions through transformation, guiding me in ways I never expected.

My passion for the metaphysical arts and the occult made *Crossing the Threshold* and navigating my *Road of Trials* less daunting. Tarot, in particular, provided a structured framework and symbolic language that helped me decode my milestones. By studying each card intensively, I uncovered their personal significance, weaving together an analysis that validated my self-awareness, deepened my individuality, and revealed meaning even in my most challenging trials.

I hope you're enjoying how Tarot storytelling aligns so beautifully with our inward journey. Its accuracy in mirroring life's experiences still amazes me. Tarot transcends the personal, tapping into universal archetypes and energies that connect us all. Whether you're familiar with

Tarot or just beginning to explore, its wisdom is a gift I feel blessed to share.

While this isn't a book about Tarot, it has been a cornerstone of my self-exploration. Its archetypes and narratives have provided clarity and guidance, shaping my path in profound ways. That's why I'm passionate about sharing how this transformative tool has empowered my growth—because if it could illuminate my way, it might just do the same for you.

If you're curious about how Tarot can illuminate your journey, I invite you to explore *The Lantern*—our very own Tarot oracle, designed to enhance your shadow work exploration with focused illuminations. It merges the best of both worlds, blending Tarot and Oracle wisdom into a tool that is soft and simplified, yet deep, inquisitive, and transformational.

THE LANTERN TAROT ORACLE:
Journey Within Illuminations

A minimalistic, divinely guided 130-card tarot oracle deck designed for deep introspection, self-discovery, and inspired action. Seamlessly blending tarot wisdom with oracle insights, this illuminating deck serves as a powerful tool for shadow work and personal transformation.

Accompanied by a comprehensive guidebook, The Lantern Tarot Oracle invites seekers to deepen their self-knowledge, embrace radical self-love, and navigate their personal Journey Within's sacred path with clarity and empowerment.

Use discount code JOURNEYWITHIN for a 10% OFF

HERO'S MILESTONE 7
Facing Tests, Allies, and Enemies

Now, circling back to an important milestone for the Hero along the Road of Trials: Facing Tests, Allies, and Enemies. This is the stage where the Hero encounters various challenges that test their strength, resilience, and resolve. It's also where they meet allies who offer support, wisdom, and guidance, as well as enemies who present obstacles and force them to confront their fears and limitations.

This stage challenges the Hero to navigate a labyrinth of obstacles, testing their commitment, determination, and willpower.

The 'Tests' aspect of this milestone is often overlooked, yet it is the crucible in which the Hero is truly forged. These trials manifest in both internal and external forms. Internally, the Hero is confronted with self-doubt, emotional triggers, and the pull of old patterns that threaten to derail progress. Externally, they must navigate difficult relationships, recognize toxic dynamics, and resist the pressures that seek to keep them small. Every test demands a choice: succumb to fear and limitation or rise with clarity and intention. It is through these moments that the Hero refines their willpower and deepens their self-trust.

Internal struggles and external conflicting forces rise to the surface, demanding that the Hero confront fears, doubts, and adversaries, while also seeking strength in allies and uncovering hidden reserves of inner power.

APPLICATION

In Tarot, this journey is vividly represented by the Chariot card. The Chariot embodies the Hero's resolve to take control of their destiny, wearing his protective armor, balancing opposing forces to move forward with intention and purpose. The two sphinxes or horses often depicted in the Chariot symbolize dualities—light and shadow, intuition and logic, chaos and order—pulling in different directions. The Hero must master these energies, harmonizing them to maintain control and stay on the path.

The Tests, Allies, and Enemies phase also highlights the Hero's need to discern who or what supports their growth versus what hinders it. Allies may come in the form of mentors, friends, or unexpected sources of wisdom, while Enemies often reflect the Hero's inner doubts, unresolved wounds, or external systems of control. This dynamic interplay challenges the Hero to refine their judgment, cultivate resilience, and develop the willpower necessary to steer through turbulent waters.

When we think of allies and enemies, we often look outward. However, one of the most crucial realizations during this phase is that we are both our own greatest ally and our worst enemy. Self-sabotage can arise if we fail to step out of our own way, allowing fears, doubts, or limiting beliefs to derail progress. Recognizing and addressing these internal conflicts is as important as managing external challenges.

Another Tarot card that resonates with the Tests, Allies, and Enemies phase is The Lovers. While often misinterpreted as solely representing romantic relationships, The Lovers card delves deeper into the theme of relationships—primarily the one we have with ourselves. It calls attention to the choices we make and the alignment of our actions with our values and desires.

The Lovers symbolize relationships, choices, and harmony. At this stage of the Hero's journey, the Hero encounters allies—connections and partnerships that genuinely support their growth—and enemies, which may manifest as external challenges or internal doubts. These encounters reflect the Hero's inner world, emphasizing trust, betrayal, cooperation, and discernment.

This phase is fundamentally about learning to build and maintain meaningful relationships, navigating challenges, and understanding the delicate balance between dependence and independence. It encourages the Hero to examine their connections with others and their inner dialogue, ensuring that their choices and relationships align with their higher purpose.

This theme of discernment and alignment with one's true self was one I struggled with firsthand, particularly in my relationships. While The Lovers card speaks to external connections, it also reflects the internal harmony—or discord—that shapes our interactions. I found that my greatest conflicts arose not just from the people around me but from the parts of myself I had yet to integrate.

For me, this milestone "Test, Allies and Enemies" of the Hero's journey was particularly confusing and very hard to navigate. Relationships—whether romantic, platonic, or professional—have always posed a significant challenge. I struggled to connect with others, establish trust, and allow for true heart-to-heart connections.

APPLICATION

Living on the spectrum usually turns normal social situations into an obstacle course.

I also encountered difficulties in letting go and closing cycles. I noticed that my empathic nature, combined with an underlying fear of abandonment and rejection, often led me to lose myself in relationships. Unknowingly, I would bind myself to others, attempting to "heal" or "fix" their issues.

This pattern caused severe energetic depletion, scattering, and fragmentation. I realized I needed not only to cut energetic cords with my past but also to reclaim the energy I had given away. I was attracting wounded or toxic connections, including people with narcissistic agendas, who drained my time, energy, and resources. To break free, I had to cultivate discernment, embrace personal accountability, and establish strong boundaries.

I am deeply sensitive to smells, sounds, lights, crowds, and certain foods, which makes socializing and casual gatherings incredibly difficult. In the past, I would put myself in awkward and uncomfortable situations in the name of people-pleasing or trying to fit in—loud crowds, flashing lights, special effects at concerts, overstimulating non-ventilated restaurants, heavy-smelling perfumes, and nightclub outings often left me overwhelmed or triggered into panic attacks from sensory overload.

Through therapy, I began to recognize social triggers and neurodivergent patterns. Situations otherwise considered "normal" to others, are truly detrimental for me. Being professionally diagnosed on the autistic spectrum brought everything into perspective, allowing radical self-love to kick-in. This self-realization not only simplified my life but also strengthened my identity. I was no longer the "weirdo" crying in restaurant bathrooms or fleeing from networking events. I no longer needed to pretend or fit into environments that drained me.

This awareness empowered me to avoid placing myself in unnecessary and unfair situations. I learned to say no to compromising invitations and peer pressure. I no longer felt the need to explain or justify my boundaries, nor did I fear rejection or judgment. I embraced my sensitivities as strengths, guides that taught me how to navigate the world more compassionately and authentically.

This transformation allowed me to cultivate a deeper relationship with myself. Through self-love and ongoing shadow work, I began to see myself as worthy and whole, even amidst my imperfections. While I am still a work-in-progress, each layer I peel back reveals more treasures within me. The more I heal, the more I love myself.

But even as I grew stronger in other areas of my life, one trial loomed larger than all others: the journey of love. Romantic relationships became my greatest ordeal—the one challenge that felt like the straw that could break the camel's back. It tested every ounce of my growth and courage, confronting me with wounds I had yet to heal and truths I had yet to face.

Yet, if the Hero's journey has taught me anything, it is that even the hardest trials are teachers—pushing us toward the deepest healing and the most profound self-love. Love, in all its forms, remains the greatest test of my resilience. But rather than seeing it as an ordeal to survive, I now recognize it as the ultimate invitation—to trust, to surrender, and to embrace my wholeness without fear.

ILLUMINATION

The Grotto transcends physical boundaries; it's not a physical space, but the setting or state where you feel safe enough to explore your depths and where vulnerability, courage, and transformation converge. It is a sacred space where shadows are faced, clarity is sought, and wounds begin their transmutation into wisdom.

Whether it's a therapy session, a Reiki healing, or the quiet corner of your room with a journal in hand, the Grotto invites you to step inward and initiate the alchemy of wounds into self-realization.

Here are a few real-life examples of the Grotto in different contexts:

In Therapy: The grotto is the therapist's office or the mental space created during a session.

- Experience: You walk into the therapist's office, where the environment feels calm yet vulnerable. As the session begins, the therapist asks a question that digs deep, triggering emotions you've suppressed for years. You feel exposed but safe enough to share the memories, thoughts, or beliefs you've avoided facing. The conversation becomes a sacred space where raw truths are explored.

JOURNEY WITHIN: DYNAMICS OF SHADOW WORK

- Purpose of the Grotto: To hold the space for you to examine patterns, emotions, and wounds without judgment. The therapist is like a guide holding a lantern in this grotto, illuminating paths you didn't know existed.

During Reiki Healing: The grotto is the energetic space created by the practitioner and the session's atmosphere.

- Experience: As you lie on the table with your eyes closed, the practitioner channels energy into specific areas of your body. You feel warmth or tingling as old energy patterns rise to the surface. Memories or emotions tied to past wounds may suddenly emerge. The space feels intimate and sacred, allowing you to release without fear of being overwhelmed.

- Purpose of the Grotto: To provide a tranquil energetic container where your body and spirit can align, heal, and integrate suppressed emotions or blockages.

When Journaling: The grotto is the quiet moment with your journal, where words become the flashlight into your inner world.

- Experience: You sit in solitude, pen in hand, and start writing about your day. As you delve deeper, unexpected feelings surface—resentment toward someone, grief over a past event, or even joy you've ignored. The page becomes a mirror reflecting parts of yourself you hadn't seen clearly. It feels raw but cathartic, like you're emptying a heavy emotional backpack.

APPLICATION

- Purpose of the Grotto: To create a private, non-judgmental space where your thoughts and emotions can be safely externalized and explored.

In Meditation: The grotto is the inner silence or visualization where the unconscious mind emerges.

- Experience: You sit in meditation, focusing on your breath. As your thoughts quiet, a vivid image of a memory or fear arises. You feel discomfort but stay present with it. The meditation space feels like a cave where shadows lurk but where clarity and insight also begin to form.
- Purpose of the Grotto: To allow you to observe and process subconscious material without reacting to it, fostering self-awareness and inner peace.

Guided Shadow Work Exercises: The grotto is the space created when you intentionally explore your fears, insecurities, or unresolved emotions.

- Experience: As you write or answer shadow work prompts, an old memory resurfaces—a time when you felt shame for being vulnerable. It's uncomfortable, but as you dig deeper, you start to connect dots about how that memory has shaped your behaviors.
- Purpose of the Grotto: To provide a contained environment for safely confronting and understanding parts of yourself you've denied or avoided.

JOURNEY WITHIN: DYNAMICS OF SHADOW WORK

In Yoga Practice: The grotto is the stillness in certain poses where emotions and energy stagnation surface.

- Experience: In a deep heart-opening pose, you suddenly feel the urge to cry without knowing why. Memories of past emotional pain come flooding back, unbidden but undeniable. You breathe through it, staying present as the sensations and emotions rise and dissipate.
- Purpose of the Grotto: To create a physical space where emotional or energetic release can occur, freeing your body and spirit from old constraints.

During a Tarot Reading: The grotto is the reflective state evoked when interpreting the cards' messages.

- Experience: A spread reveals cards like The Moon. You're confronted with truths about illusions in your life that you've been avoiding. The cards serve as a mirror, guiding you to explore the deeper meaning of events or patterns you're experiencing.
- Purpose of the Grotto: To provide a symbolic framework for uncovering hidden truths and finding guidance within the chaos of your journey.

APPLICATION

In Everyday Reflection: The grotto is the mental or emotional space created when you pause and honestly assess your life.

- Experience: On a quiet evening, you find yourself replaying a conflict from the day. Instead of blaming others, you ask yourself: Why did this upset me so much? What part of me is hurting? As you sit with discomfort, a deeper wound—perhaps a childhood fear of rejection—becomes clear.
- Purpose of the Grotto: To encourage moments of introspection that lead to self-discovery and emotional integration.

Know Thyself: Introspections 075

75. The Grotto: What part of my inner world am I most resistant to exploring, and what might be waiting for me there?

PHASE V
Alchemizing Your Wounds

By the age of 40, I became a single mom, choosing to walk away from a loveless marriage. I decided it was time to show my son what an empowered, authentic, and truly happy mother looked like. For both our sakes, I made the decision to break free from a life that no longer reflected my truth.

Having my son is, without a doubt, the purest manifestation of love I have ever experienced. Romantic love, however, was uncharted territory for me. Growing up, I never saw healthy affection between my parents; displays of love or tenderness were nonexistent. If I'm being honest, I had never witnessed a relationship where two people truly honored one another with love, devotion, faithfulness, and genuine commitment.

Instead, I carried the wounds of my father's infidelity against my mother, which led me to expect or suspect betrayal in every relationship. I internalized the idea of marriage as a kind of oppression—a trap for women who would inevitably become servants to their spouses. Falling in love, from what I'd observed, seemed to strip people of their strength and intelligence, leaving them vulnerable and dependent.

Because of this, I never allowed myself to truly fall in love. Although it was easy for me to perform the role of a straight woman—sometimes bicurious or even bisexual—being in a superficial relationship with a man felt safer. It guaranteed emotional distance, ensuring I wouldn't risk falling in love or experiencing the pain that often seemed to follow.

The truth was, no man had ever truly moved me. My pretend relationships were a form of protection, a shield I used to keep my heart untouched and my independence intact.

Despite my efforts to avoid love, I always craved romantic connection—knee-bending passion and someone who could take my breath away. So, when I finally came out "officially" and embraced my most authentic self, I set out in search of my true love's kiss.

I opened myself to dating and meeting new people—sometimes to my own detriment. To my surprise, a part of me secretly yearned to fall in love and believed I was doing all the right things to manifest it. This time, I was dating women, which felt aligned with my truth. I put myself out there wholeheartedly, hoping to find "the one." But what I failed to see was that I was still attracting pretend relationships. Though I had finally—courageously—chosen the "right gender," I was still operating from fear and stuck in the wrong paradigm.

APPLICATION

JOURNEY WITHIN DOORWAY #7:
The Dagger (Hurt, Chaos, and the Catalyst for Change)

Deep inside the Grotto, beneath the innermost layers of our being, lies *The Dagger*—the source of our deepest, most unexpected wound. This is not just any pain; it is the wound that shapes our shadows, affecting every part of our psyche. The Dagger is both the weapon that inflicts hurt and the tool that holds the power to sever the old self. Pulling it out is the ultimate act of liberation, the key to transformation. Once removed, we are forced to confront what lies beneath—the root of all imbalance, the core of our suffering.

Though we may encounter many Daggers in life, there is one that cuts the deepest. It is the wound that lingers, shaping our entire reality. It is the catalyst of our shadow self, calling us to awareness, healing, and eventual transformation.

For me, that Dagger wasn't merely the absence of self-love—it was the very belief that I was unworthy of it. The weight of years of programming, the oppressive narratives of the Hierophant Shadow—all reinforced this deep sense of unworthiness. This belief poisoned my ability to receive love, because I couldn't fathom that I was deserving of it. Fading imprints and pulsating echoes from my parents, society, and religious dogma only validated the subconscious excuses I created to justify this belief. My core wound was clear: *Unworthiness.*

I had become the gay, witch, tarot-reading "child of Satan" as my parents and society had conditioned me to believe. This narrative wasn't just an external judgment—it embedded itself into my bones, shaping my perception of self and my place in the world. It was a lie, but for far too long, it was *my truth.*

My core wound had me utterly convinced—on both a subconscious and superconscious level—that I was unlovable and inherently unworthy of love, not even my own. This belief fostered a deep sense of self-hatred, which manifested in countless expressions of self-sabotage, keeping me trapped in a cycle of pain and rejection that I unknowingly perpetuated.

This deeply ingrained belief system shaped my reality, compelling me to choose pretend relationships as both a shield and a confirmation of my unworthiness. These connections served to protect me from the vulnerability of true intimacy while simultaneously validating the narrative that I was undeserving of real love.

But shields are not impenetrable, and cracks began to form. There were moments when love nearly broke through—when someone's tenderness felt too real, too close to the truth I was afraid to face. Each time, I found a way to sabotage it, to prove to myself that I was right to remain guarded. I told myself that I was in control, but in reality, fear was still the one holding the reins.

It was a never-ending cycle—safely distant from connection, yet painfully entrenched in a prison of my own making.

In astrology, the planet Chiron represents our deepest wound and the path toward healing it. Known as the *Wounded Healer,* Chiron's placement in our natal chart

APPLICATION

reveals where our core wounds lie—often rooted in childhood experiences, past traumas, or karmic patterns—and where we have the potential for profound healing and transformation.

In my chart, Chiron sits in Taurus, highlighting a deep wound around self-worth and personal value, particularly tied to identity. No surprise there, right? It feels like it's right on target—and quite intentional from the Universe's design perspective. It's like a master plan, choosing the right elements for my chart and the right parents or upbringings to activate them.

Yet luckily for me, I also had the antidote—Chiron's medicine. Also in Taurus.

Understanding this wound through the lens of Chiron gave me a new perspective. It wasn't just about my past or failed relationships; it was a karmic imprint that had influenced my entire sense of self-worth. Shadow work had already exposed my patterns, but astrology offered a map—a cosmic confirmation that this wound was not random. It was something my soul had chosen to experience, alchemize, and eventually transcend.

I share this insight because I believe that intentional shadow work—meaning, focused on a specific angle like exploring our Chiron influence, or other aspects of our chart such as the North Node, our Big 3, or our Venus—can illuminate how our wounds manifest in our lives.

More importantly, it shows us how to harvest the ingredients for the "medicine" or "antidote"—figuratively speaking—and alchemize the wound into gifts of wisdom, compassion, and strength.

JOURNEY WITHIN: DYNAMICS OF SHADOW WORK

The goal of working with Chiron's shadow is to transform the wound into a source of healing, inspiration, and service, allowing us to step into our fullest potential:

- **Self-Compassion:** Accept your pain as part of your humanity.
- **Transcendence:** Turn your experience into wisdom that guides others.
- **Empowerment:** Reclaim the parts of yourself that were lost due to the wound.

The Dagger represents the pain, wound, or shadow aspect that demands healing. It is a divine instrument of chaos, intentionally designed to disrupt the status quo and redirect your focus to the unaddressed aspects of your being. This is not arbitrary pain; it is purposeful and often soul-directed, guiding you toward the fulfillment of your higher purpose.

While I can't say for certain if there's only one Dagger, I can confidently share that each of us carries a unique primary Dagger—shaped by our individual life lessons, blueprints, and soul missions. One person's Dagger may stem from abandonment, while another's may be forged from betrayal, fear, or shame.

Each Dagger mirrors the soul's journey, revealing the lessons and challenges that require attention. Whether shaped by abandonment, fear, shame, or betrayal, the Dagger's role is to liberate, not harm. It directs you straight to the wound, whispering: *"This is where you must look."*

APPLICATION

Confronting the Dagger through shadow work is a portal for healing, empowerment, and soul reclamation. It is painful—but it is also the most liberating act of self-love.

Each wound revealed is an invitation to reclaim suppressed fragments of your soul. And this reclamation ultimately leads to clarity, resilience, and the alchemical transformation of pain into power.

HERO'S MILESTONE 8
Accessing the Innermost

Accessing the innermost part of ourselves is one of the most profound milestones in the Hero's Journey. It is the moment when we pierce through layers of illusion, conditioning, and fear, arriving at the raw, unfiltered truth of who we are. This stage is about deep introspection, surrender, and courage. It is where we move beyond the surface and step into the sacred space of our true essence.

This experience can feel like stepping into the unknown—confronting the parts of yourself that have been hidden, denied, or repressed. It may feel like an unraveling, a moment where the weight of the past surfaces in full force. But within this space of vulnerability lies the power of true self-awareness and liberation. This is where healing takes root, where illusions dissolve, and where you come face to face with your innermost truth.

The deeper you go, the more you realize that this process is not about fixing yourself, but about remembering. Remembering who you are beyond societal expectations, past wounds, and self-imposed limitations. It is about reclaiming the parts of yourself that you have buried and integrating them into your wholeness.

As you access this space, the transformation begins. You start to see patterns that have shaped your behaviors, relationships, and choices. You recognize the weight of old programming and belief systems. And in this space

APPLICATION

of recognition, a choice emerges: to continue carrying what no longer serves you, or to release it and embrace the new.

This process is sacred, personal, and deeply transformative. It is not just a moment but a passage—a bridge between who you were and who you are becoming. And once you step into this space, there is no turning back. You have answered the call to awaken.

As you stand at this threshold, ask yourself: What is my deepest wound trying to teach me? What truth have I been avoiding, and how can I reclaim my power from it? Remember, accessing your innermost self is not about perfection—it is about presence. It is about holding space for all that you are, without shame or resistance. The deeper you go, the more you realize that your healing is not about becoming someone new—it's about becoming who you've always been.

SECTION 22. THE ALCHEMY PROCESS

Alchemy, in its historical and philosophical essence, is the transformation of raw or base materials into something refined, purified, and elevated. While medieval alchemists sought to turn lead into gold, the deeper, esoteric meaning of alchemy has always been about inner transformation, self-mastery, and spiritual evolution.

In shadow work, alchemy is the sacred transmutation of wounds, limiting beliefs, and buried pain into wisdom, empowerment, and self-actualization. This transformation unfolds deep within the **grotto or innermost—the hidden chambers of the self—**where we sit with our wounds, not to suffer, but to heal and transmute.

Beneath the dagger—the pain, trauma, and conditioning—lies the wound, or wounding, a raw and unprocessed energy buried in the subconscious. Alchemy is not about erasing the wound but about meeting it, understanding it, shifting and reshaping its essence.

Just as alchemists refined materials in hidden chambers, shadow work happens in the grotto—the inner sanctum of transformation. The dagger, a symbol of past pain, is not meant to harm but to be wielded with awareness. The wound beneath it is not a weakness but a portal to evolution.

True alchemy in shadow work is not about escaping pain but transmuting it into wisdom, resilience, power and liberation. When we engage at this level, we become the alchemists of our own evolution, turning past wounds into personal power.

The process begins with *Calcination*, where we burn away the old, the unnecessary, and what no longer serves us. This phase is all about letting go of ego, false beliefs, and attachments that hold us back. It's like clearing the clutter from your life—whether that's outdated thinking or harmful habits—so you can make room for something new. The purpose is to strip away the impurities to reveal your true, authentic self.

1. **Calcination (Keyword: Purification)** — The burning away of ego and attachments, reducing the self to ashes. It represents humility and breaking down illusions. Calcination represents the first stage in the alchemical process, where the unnecessary and inauthentic are destroyed to reveal the essence of who we truly are.

    - **Shadow Work Insight:** The beginning of shadow work requires confronting the ego and burning away illusions, false beliefs, and attachments that no longer serve you.

    - **Sequence:** This is the initiation phase, where the fire of self-awareness begins to cleanse and reveal what lies beneath.

Once the old has been burned away, we enter *Dissolution*, where the structures and forms of the former self are dismantled. In this phase, we start to break down and dissolve limiting beliefs and patterns that kept us confined to a certain way of being. It's like taking apart the walls you've built around yourself, releasing everything that's rigid and constricted so that your soul can expand and flow freely.

2. **Dissolution (Keyword: Dismantle)** — Dissolving and breaking down old patterns, beliefs, emotions and structures into a formless state. This stage allows for deeper reflection and emotional release.

   - **Shadow Work Insight:** After burning away the surface, deep emotions and hidden aspects of the subconscious emerge. Old identities and beliefs dissolve, leaving you in a raw and vulnerable state.

   - **Sequence:** This phase encourages the release of control, allowing buried feelings and suppressed aspects of yourself to surface for examination.

After dissolving the old, we go through *Separation*, where we carefully sort and discern what is truly ours versus what we've inherited or absorbed from outside influences, like society or family. In this phase, we separate the authentic from the inauthentic, identifying which beliefs, values, and behaviors resonate with our true self and which ones need to be discarded. This process helps you get clear on who you really are, free from external noise.

3. **Separation (Keyword: Discernment)** — Identifying and separating what is pure and valuable from what no longer serves. It's a process of filtering and refining. Separation calls for careful discernment, keeping only what serves the soul's journey.

- **Shadow Work Insight:** Now, you sift through what has emerged, discerning what is essential and aligned with your truth versus what needs to be let go.
- **Sequence:** This is a critical moment of sorting and reflection, where clarity begins to form about your core essence.

Once we've separated what no longer serves, we move into *Conjunction*, where we begin to integrate the parts of ourselves that were previously fragmented. Here, we bring together all the healed, released, and clarified aspects of ourselves—our shadow and light—into a unified whole. It's the phase where we fuse all the parts of us that are in alignment with our true self, creating a harmonious balance between mind, body, and spirit.

4. **Conjunction (Keyword: Fusion)** — The integration of opposites to form a unified whole. This is the balance of masculine and feminine energies or shadow and light. Represents union and synthesis, combining elements harmoniously, creating a stronger whole.
   - **Shadow Work Insight:** Here, opposites within you are integrated—light and shadow, masculine and feminine, higher self and wounded self. This is the beginning of inner harmony and balance.
   - **Sequence:** The integration phase, where fragmentation gives way to wholeness.

With all parts now integrated, we enter *Fermentation*, the phase of deep internal change. This is the stage where we undergo true metamorphosis—a radical shift in our being. It's like the process of fermentation, where something is transformed into something else, often in a way that feels mysterious or even uncomfortable. We let go of old beliefs, relationships, and habits, allowing ourselves to be reborn into a more authentic version of who we are.

5. **Fermentation (Keyword: Metamorphosis)** — The stage of inspiration and spiritual rebirth, where divine essence begins to infuse the work. This phase reflects profound inner change and transformation, as the process of growth (or rebirth) after decay.

    - **Shadow Work Insight:** As integration settles, inspiration and spiritual transformation take root. This stage is about spiritual rebirth, allowing your higher self to guide the process.

    - **Sequence:** The moment of evolution, where the energy of shadow work catalyzes profound personal growth.

After fermentation, we enter *Distillation*, where we begin to refine and clarify the essence of who we are. This phase involves stripping away any remaining impurities and focusing on our highest potential. We become clearer and more precise in our thinking and actions, and we shed any remaining layers of self-doubt or confusion. It's a process of polishing ourselves to embody our highest expression.

6. **Distillation (Keyword: Refinement)** — Refining and purifying the spirit, leading to greater clarity and alignment with higher truths. Through distillation's purification one gains clarity, focus, and spiritual elevation.

   - **Shadow Work Insight:** The spirit is refined, as clarity and purity emerge. This stage emphasizes aligning actions, thoughts, and beliefs with your authentic self.
   - **Sequence:** The polishing phase, where you shed remaining distortions and step into greater alignment with your truth.

Finally, we reach *Coagulation*, where everything comes together. This is the culmination of the alchemical process: we are fully transformed, and our soul's purpose is now clear. In this phase, we embody our true self and live in alignment with our higher calling. It's about stepping into your full power, knowing who you are, and bringing your authentic self into the world. You've completed the alchemical process and are now fully whole, integrated, and able to manifest your deepest desires.

7. **Coagulation (Keyword: Completion)** — The final stage of realization and embodiment of the Philosopher's Stone, symbolizing ultimate self-mastery, spiritual wholeness and solidifying wisdom into a new reality. Coagulation is the final step of alchemical transformation, embodying fulfillment.

- **Shadow Work Insight:** The final stage represents wholeness and the embodiment of self-mastery. You've transmuted shadow into light and achieved a grounded, integrated self.
- **Sequence:** The culmination phase, where the Philosopher's Stone—the realization of your limitless potential—is embodied.

Summary:

In simple sequence, the alchemical journey is a process of inner transformation that starts by shedding what doesn't serve us (Calcination), dismantling the old patterns (Dissolution), and discerning what is truly ours (Separation). Then, we integrate our authentic self (Conjunction), undergo a deep internal metamorphosis (Fermentation), refine and clarify our essence (Distillation), and finally manifest our true self into the world (Coagulation). This alchemical path is all about personal growth, self-realization, and transformation.

As a whole process this sequence mirrors the natural progression of shadow work:

- Awareness and Release (Calcination & Dissolution),
- Understanding and Integration (Separation & Conjunction),
- Transformation and Embodiment (Fermentation, Distillation, & Coagulation).

APPLICATION

Beneath the Dagger lies our core wound, which deeply affects the flow and balance of our chakra system. Each core wound often manifests as an imbalance or blockage in one or more chakras, disrupting the energy flow that governs our physical, emotional, and spiritual health.

When we address our core wounds, we not only clear these blockages but also restore the free flow of energy, bringing healing and harmony to our entire being. This process helps us align more fully with our authentic selves, enabling growth, clarity, and empowerment.

The next chakra specific **Know Thyself** self-assessment questions will help you identify where your core wound may be affecting your energy system, providing insight into areas needing healing and attention.

E-COURSE LECTURE: "Facing Our Core Wound"

Know Thyself: Introspections 076-082

CORE WOUND

76. Root Chakra (Muladhara): What foundational belief about safety, security, or belonging is rooted in my core wound, and how can I nurture a sense of stability and trust within myself?

77. Sacral Chakra (Svadhisthana): How has my core wound affected my ability to experience joy, creativity, or emotional connection, and what would it look like to embrace pleasure and emotional flow in a healthy, authentic way?

78. Solar Plexus Chakra (Manipura): What fears or limiting beliefs about my power and self-worth have been shaped by my core wound, and how can I reclaim my confidence and sense of autonomy?

79. Heart Chakra (Anahata): How has my core wound influenced my ability to give and receive love, and what can I do to open my heart to deeper compassion and connection?

80. Throat Chakra (Vishuddha): In what ways has my core wound silenced my voice or truth, and how can I begin to express myself more authentically and without fear?

81. Third Eye Chakra (Ajna): How has my core wound distorted my inner vision or intuition, and what practices can I cultivate to trust my inner wisdom and see myself and my life more clearly?

82. Crown Chakra (Sahasrara): How has my core wound disconnected me from a sense of higher purpose or universal connection, and how can I align with divine flow and spiritual trust?

HERO'S MILESTONE 9
Experiencing the Ordeal

In Tarot storytelling, facing our core wound is depicted as encountering The Ordeal.

The Ordeal is the fire that purifies, the storm that breaks and rebuilds, the abyss that forces transformation. In the Hero's Journey, this is the moment of deepest challenge—pulling the dagger out and facing the core wound, the unhealed trauma, and the darkest parts of the psyche.

This experience is raw, intense, and often painful. It can feel like a breakdown, an unraveling of everything you thought you knew. The illusions that once provided comfort are stripped away, leaving you face to face with your deepest fears and unresolved wounds. The Ordeal forces you to confront the very thing you have avoided—the old wounds that dictate your patterns, your self-worth, and your ability to step into your full power.

It is in this fire that you are tested. Will you retreat, or will you surrender to the process? The flames of transformation burn away what no longer serves you—the fears, the attachments, the false identities. This is not destruction for the sake of suffering; it is purification. Just as the Phoenix must burn to rise anew, you too must release what is compromised, unhealed, and misaligned in order to emerge as something greater. This is your alchemy process.

The Ordeal is not about suffering—it is about breakthrough. It is the initiation into a new version of yourself, one that is stronger, wiser, and more aligned with your authentic essence. But just as the Phoenix, after rising, must learn to spread its wings anew, you too must adjust to this new reality. The recalibration that follows is just as important as the transformation itself.

Not everyone will be able to cross this bridge with you. Not everyone will understand your journey, and some may resist or reject the version of you that emerges from the fire. That is part of the process. The Ordeal teaches discernment—who and what aligns with your new self, and what must be left behind.

This is the defining moment of your journey—the moment where you claim yourself, in full authenticity, no longer bound by the chains of the past. And as you step forward, you do so with the wisdom, strength, and clarity forged in the fire of your own transformation.

Experiencing The Ordeal and confronting our core wounds will truly test and strengthen your character. Your evolution is sacred, and this passage through the Bridge is one of the most defining moments of your journey. And I can't wait to walk with you through it!

My personal experience of The Ordeal was deeply emotional. And I say this with pride and joy, considering I wasn't able to process emotions when I first began my journey. I learned that the inward journey is not linear but rather a spiral, where healing deepens and expands with each cycle. Embracing this process, with all its layers and complexities, allows for continual growth—illuminating your shadows, integrating your lessons, and reclaiming your wholeness.

APPLICATION

While we generally tackle one issue at a time, the interconnectedness of our psyche means that when we heal at one level, we invite healing in other aspects of our being—whether in our relationships, careers, finances, health, or emotional states. The process may unfold incrementally, but the ripple effects bring profound relief and clarity, gradually unblocking stuck energy and fostering greater balance.

We all carry daggers and deep wounds. Shadow work isn't a one-time event; it's a journey of peeling back layers, confronting old wounds, and discovering the healing we once thought impossible. Some days will feel like setbacks, but each confrontation with our shadows is an act of self-love—a step toward reclaiming our true essence.

It is essential to clarify that shadow work is not about fixing yourself—because you are not broken. It's about rediscovering who you truly are beneath the layers of conditioning, fear, and self-doubt. It's about remembering the truth of your being and embracing the fullness of your humanity.

As I continued to navigate my shadows, I began to heal not only from past trauma but also from the societal conditioning that had shaped me into someone afraid to be fully seen, loved, and accepted. I began to recognize the power of vulnerability, the depths in tears, the beauty in imperfection, and the strength that comes from surrendering to my authentic self.

By acknowledging and embracing my shadows, I stopped running from my fears and avoiding my emotions. Instead, I faced them head-on with courage and compassion, understanding that each step of this journey was an act of self-love. This act of self-love became my greatest tool for healing, transformation, and empowerment.

The Ordeal is your invitation. Step forward, not because you have no fear, but because your truth is greater than your doubt. Trust that what awaits you is not just survival—it is your becoming.

ILLUMINATION

The Dagger represents the embodiment of your deepest pain—the scar that refuses to heal, the weight you carry even when you are unaware of it. You may think the Dagger caused the wounding, but in truth, it was the wound that shaped the Dagger. The Dagger is a physical manifestation of the pain itself—like a pushpin on a map, marking the exact location where your soul needs tending. It can be pulled out, not to destroy, but to reveal what lies beneath.

Let me attempt to cast a visual of this symbology. How can I describe a weapon that causes pain yet also becomes the very handle that will stop it?

If we must describe it to satisfy the senses, we might envision the Dagger as a sharp, gleaming blade—that draws your eye, impossible to ignore, even when you try to look away. It's honed to perfection. Ancient. Forged in the depths of your own psyche, with a deadly edge that reflects both your light and your shadows. It hums with eerie energy, vibrating with the weight of its pain.

At first, the metal is impossibly cold—unfeeling and distant, like the pain you've numbed or forgotten. But when you gaze upon it, when your fingers dare to wrap around it, it shifts—warming, awakening, demanding to be felt. It doesn't burn the skin, but it presses into the soul with an unnerving heat that lingers beneath the surface.

The handle is neither elegant nor comforting, yet strangely familiar. It fits in your hand with a weight that feels both unnatural and essential. When you touch it, there's a magnetic pull—a subtle tug on your soul, drawing you closer to the wound it represents. You can feel its power coursing through you, a heavy, unspoken connection that's impossible to sever—like a tether binding you to past versions of yourself.

The pain you feel isn't just physical—it's the aching presence of unhealed wounds, the things you've carried in silence for far too long. Every move you make with it inside you sends ripples through your body, affecting your thoughts, emotions, and the way you view the world. It is an anchor—one that roots you in the past, reminding you that what you've endured can never be fully escaped until it is brought to the surface and released.

When you finally attempt to pull it out, the act feels almost impossibly difficult—not just because of the pain, but because of the fear. The Dagger has lived inside you for so long that its absence feels more unsettling than its presence. Pain, after all, becomes familiar. Predictable. A shield as much as a wound. But removing it means facing what lies beneath—the rawness, the vulnerability, the unknown. And yet, it is only through this courageous removal that true healing can begin.

The moment the Dagger is withdrawn, there is a rush—a deep exhale, a surge of energy, as if the very world shifts with you. Yet the emptiness left in its wake is undeniable. It's raw, exposed, vulnerable. But this hollow space is sacred—because it is where your true self is meant to rise. And though the scar may remain, the power it once held over you dissolves.

The Dagger does not seek to destroy you. It waits to be acknowledged, understood, and ultimately—removed. In its place, something new emerges: self-recognition, the quiet power of sovereignty, and the radiant clarity of a soul no longer at war with itself.

APPLICATION

 Know Thyself: Introspections 083

83. The Dagger: What (recurring) emotional pain or limiting belief do I carry, and how is it shaping my life and choices?

ILLUMINATION
ALCHEMY PROCESS
Unfolding Timeline

PART 1 OF 3

The Bench (Contemplation)

- **Stage:** Pre-Alchemy (Preparation)
- **Where It Happens:** Outside the transformative space.
- **Purpose:** This is the soul's moment of stillness, where imbalance and shadows first come into focus. It's the preparation and conscious acknowledgment of the need for transformation.

The Sanctuary (Devotion)

- **Stage:** Pre-Alchemy (Commitment)
- **Where It Happens:** Outside the Grotto, at the threshold.
- **Purpose:** A sacred dedication to begin the inward journey. This marks the decision to step into shadow work and nurture a safe container for transformation.

APPLICATION

The Lantern (Consciousness)

- **Stage:** Pre-Alchemy (Illumination)
- **Where It Happens:** The entrance of the Grotto.
- **Purpose:** Lighting up your awareness to navigate through the darkness of the subconscious mind. It signifies clarity and the initial awakening of consciousness.

The Compass (Direction)

- **Stage:** Pre-Alchemy (Orientation)
- **Where It Happens:** The entrance of the Grotto, alongside the Lantern.
- **Purpose:** Activating alignment with your true north and heart's desires. The Compass sets the course for the alchemical journey ahead.

The Cloak (Protection)

- **Stage:** During Alchemy (Shielding)
- **Where It Happens:** As you step fully into the Grotto.
- **Purpose:** This is the divine protection that surrounds you during your most vulnerable moments. It ensures safety as you explore and dismantle shadow layers.

JOURNEY WITHIN: DYNAMICS OF SHADOW WORK

The Grotto (Innermost) -and- the Dagger (Wound)

- **Stage:** 80% Alchemy Process (Calcination - to - Fermentation)
- **Where It Happens:** Deep within, at the core of your being.
- **Purpose:** The sacred chamber where all layers are stripped back, allowing the alchemy process to unfold.
- **Process:** The Dagger points to your deepest wounds and shadows. It initiates the alchemical process by exposing the source of chaos, pain, and imbalance, demanding healing and growth. The soul's essence is revealed and transformed through:
    - Calcination (Burning away illusions)
    - Dissolution (Dismantling structures)
    - Separation (Discernment of truth)
    - Conjunction (Reintegrating authentic pieces)
    - Fermentation (Allowing new growth)

APPLICATION

PART 2 OF 3

The Bridge (Recalibration)

- **Stage:** 20% Alchemy Process (Distillation - Coagulation) Post-Alchemy (Integration)
- **Where It Happens:** Exiting the Grotto.
- **Purpose:** The Bridge connects the transformed self to the external world. It filters out what no longer aligns, helping you adjust to your new frequency and integrate the changes with grace.
    - Distillation: Refining the essence.
    - Coagulation: Solidifying your true self.
- **Process:** Transition Between Fermentation and Coagulation

Bridge's position right after Fermentation and as a precursor to Coagulation makes it a critical juncture in the alchemical process.

- Fermentation is the phase of spiritual rebirth, where new awareness and potential begin to emerge after the inner work of dissolving, separating, and recombining. However, this new awareness is still in its formative stages.
- Coagulation represents the full embodiment of the new self—the solidification of wisdom, growth, and transformation into your everyday life.

The Bridge is the transition between these two phases. It's the space where:

JOURNEY WITHIN: DYNAMICS OF SHADOW WORK

- **Integration Happens:** The insights and growth from Fermentation begin to take root. You start applying these lessons to real-world scenarios, testing your readiness for embodiment.

- **Vulnerability Arises:** This is a liminal space. You are no longer who you were but haven't fully become your new self. Without intentionality, boundaries, and self-care, there's a risk of slipping back into old patterns, diluting the progress made in Fermentation.

- **Resilience is Built:** The Bridge requires active recalibration—choosing to support the new, tender aspects of your being with structure and intentionality. Boundaries and self-care become the scaffolding that ensures the changes from Fermentation are fortified, preparing you for Coagulation.

Think of the Bridge as a crucible of transformation where your resolve is tested. It's not just a passive transition but an active process of:

- Choosing the new over the old.
- Fortifying your energy and clarity.
- Bridging the gap between your inner work and the world around you.

By honoring the Bridge as a phase of recalibration and refinement, you ensure that the changes initiated in Fermentation are not only preserved but strengthened, allowing you to step fully into Coagulation with integrity and power.

APPLICATION

PART 3 OF 3

The Path (Conviction)

- **Stage:** Post-Alchemy (Alignment)
- **Where It Happens:** Beyond the Bridge.
- **Purpose:** This is where you embrace your purpose with certainty. It's the space where alignment with your true self becomes undeniable, guiding you forward with clarity.

The Summit (Achievement)

- **Stage:** Post-Alchemy (Celebration and Expansion)
- **Where It Happens:** At the apex of the journey.
- **Purpose:** The Summit is where you embody the rewards of your transformation. It's a space of celebration, reflection, and preparation for stepping fully into your power.

The Vessel (Embodiment)

- **Stage:** Final Alchemy (Coagulation)
- **Where It Happens:** After the Summit, encompassing all realms of your being.
- **Purpose:** You now hold the alchemical essence within you, embodying your authentic self and limitless potential. You are the stable yet flexible container of divine energy.

JOURNEY WITHIN: DYNAMICS OF SHADOW WORK

The Akasha (Sacred Mission)

- **Stage:** Beyond Alchemy (Higher Purpose)
- **Where It Happens:** Transcending the entire journey.
- **Purpose:** This is the overarching reason for the alchemical journey. It's your divine purpose, revealed and fulfilled as you step fully into your sacred mission, carrying the wisdom and light of your transformation.

APPLICATION

 Know Thyself: Introspections 084-090

THE ALCHEMY PROCESS

84. Calcination: What aspects of my identity or ego am I clinging to that no longer serve my growth or authenticity?

85. Dissolution: What emotional wounds or limiting beliefs am I ready to dissolve to create space for healing and transformation?

86. Separation: What truths about myself can I extract from my shadows to better understand my authentic nature?

87. Conjunction: How can I bring together my light and shadow aspects to create a harmonious and balanced sense of self?

88. Fermentation: How can I embrace the lessons of my struggles to ignite deeper spiritual growth and inner transformation?

89. Distillation: What patterns or habits can I refine to embody a clearer and more aligned version of myself?

90. Coagulation: How can I fully embrace my shadows and strengths to live as my most empowered and unified self?

ROOT OF THE SHADOW

- **The Hierophant** — Societal conditioning, authority figures, learned belief systems.
- **6 of Cups** — Past experiences, childhood wounds, nostalgia for the past.
- **The Devil** — Toxic attachments, addictions, unhealthy coping mechanisms.

ROOT OF THE SHADOW

- **The Empress** — Mother Archetype, Divine Feminine, Nurture, Creation
- **The Emperor** — Father Archetype, Divine Masculine, Authority, Discipline

 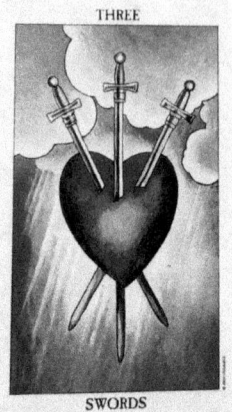 

OUR WOUNDS

- **2 of Swords** — Indecision, avoidance of truth.
- **3 of Swords** — Heartbreak, grief, emotional wounding.
- **5 of Swords** — Self-sabotage, conflict, unhealthy competition.

  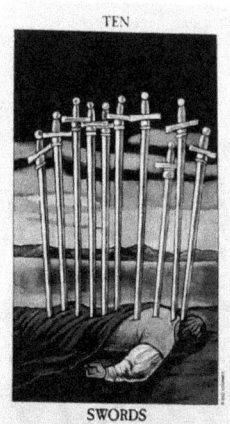

OUR WOUNDS

- **8 of Swords —** Feeling trapped, self-imposed limitations.
- **9 of Swords —** Anxiety, intrusive thoughts, sleepless nights.
- **10 of Swords —** Betrayal, loss, backstabbing.

OUR WOUNDS

- **2 of Pentacles —** Overwhelm, lack of balance, emotional juggling.
- **5 of Pentacles —** Abandonment wounds, financial or emotional loss.
- **4 of Cups —** Rejection, disappointment, disconnection, or apathy.
- **7 of Cups —** Illusions, confusion, being lost in distractions

OUR WOUNDS

- **5 of Wands** — Internal and external conflicts, ego battles.
- **10 of Wands** — Burdens, exhaustion, emotional overload.
- **The Moon** — Fears, illusions, deception of the self, subconscious blocks.
- **7 of Swords** — Deception, self-deception, avoidance.

CHAPTER FIVE
INTEGRATION

PHASE VI
Rebirth and Reclamation

In both the Hero's Journey and real life, rebirth and reclamation represent the moment when transformation becomes tangible. It is not just the realization of change but the lived experience of it—the shift from understanding to embodiment. It is not enough to survive the ordeal; one must rise from it, claim the lessons, and consciously step into a new way of being.

In Tarot storytelling, rebirth is the moment the Hero emerges from their greatest ordeal—transformed, renewed, and forever changed. Like the Phoenix rising from the ashes. This symbolic death and resurrection signify the shedding of old identities, beliefs, and limitations. Yet, transformation is not passive; it requires intentional integration.

Reclamation, on the other hand, is the Hero's conscious decision to own their transformation. It is the process of reclaiming personal power, wisdom, and agency—no longer defined by past wounds or external expectations.

In shadow work and self-mastery, rebirth happens when we transcend old patterns and step into self-awareness. However, true change is solidified through reclamation—choosing to own our healing process, embrace our wholeness, and step fully into our sovereignty.

Reclamation is the act of taking back:

- **Your Power** — No longer outsourcing validation or worth.
- **Your Truth** — Living in alignment with your deepest knowing.
- **Your Narrative** — Redefining yourself beyond past wounds or imposed identities.

It is important to clarify or emphasize that rebirth and reclamation are deeply interconnected, but one can exist without the other—though not in its fullest form.

Rebirth Without Reclamation

Rebirth is the moment of awakening—a shift in consciousness, a realization, or even a transformation initiated by an ordeal. However, if there is no reclamation, this change remains internal, untapped, or unclaimed. It becomes a potential, not a lived reality.

- **Example in the Hero's Journey:** A Hero faces death and survives, gaining wisdom and insight, but if they refuse to bring that wisdom back to the world or step into their new role, their transformation remains incomplete.
- **Example in Real Life:** Someone undergoes deep shadow work and experiences profound healing, but if they do not own their power, change their actions, or integrate their lessons, they may fall back into old cycles.

Reclamation Without Rebirth

Reclamation without rebirth is acting as if transformation has occurred without the internal shift to support it. It is claiming power without truly transmuting wounds, often leading to inauthenticity, bypassing, or a fragile sense of empowerment.

- Example in the Hero's Journey: A Hero may return home, proclaiming victory, but if they have not actually been transformed by their experiences, their return lacks true depth or wisdom.
- Example in Real Life: Someone asserts their independence, sets boundaries, or claims self-mastery, but deep down, they are still operating from fear, unhealed wounds, or unprocessed trauma. This can lead to false confidence, defensiveness, or an identity rooted in resistance rather than authentic empowerment.

The Balance: Rebirth Fuels Reclamation

For true individuation and self-mastery, rebirth and reclamation must work together:

1. Rebirth brings the awakening, insight, and transformation—a new way of seeing and being.
2. Reclamation brings embodiment, integration, and sovereignty—the conscious choice to live in alignment with that transformation.

INTEGRATION

Without reclamation, rebirth is just a fleeting realization. Without rebirth, reclamation is just an illusion. Together, they create the foundation for true, lasting self-mastery.

SECTION 23. HOW TO NAVIGATE AND SUSTAIN YOUR JOURNEY

Embarking on your shadow work journey may seem daunting, but the rewards are profound. You are not alone in this process—this path has been walked by many before you, and support is available to guide you through every step. As we reflect on what we've covered so far, let's revisit the essential foundations of starting and navigating your journey inward:

1. **First, We Decide! The first and most powerful step is choosing ourselves** — This is not just a passing thought or a passive realization—it is an active commitment to love ourselves enough to face what has been hidden, suppressed, or unacknowledged. Choosing ourselves means reclaiming our autonomy, honoring our truth, and making space for transformation. This is you on the Bench, saying YES to stepping into Sanctuary, focusing on your inner work and allowing healing to begin.

2. **Setting Clear Intentions and Establishing Significance** — When you define what you hope to achieve through shadow work, you anchor yourself in purpose. Your intentions act as a guiding light, keeping you focused when challenges arise. This mindset shift opens the door to love, healing, and transformation beyond what you can imagine.

3. **Choosing Your Approach and Holding Space for Yourself**
   — Your shadow work practice should be a safe, intentional, and sacred experience. Dedicate time, create a ritual, and cultivate a space that supports your inner work. Select a shadow work approach that resonates with you and commit to the process.

And that part—committing to self-devotion—is what makes all the difference.

That is why having support and guidance matters. This brings us to the next essential element... consider having a blueprint, an action plan, or a structured support system—something that keeps you accountable, on track, and resilient when resistance, setbacks, or self-sabotage arise.

Shadow work is not about perfection; it is about progress. It is about showing up for yourself even when it feels overwhelming; when old wounds resurface; when the shadows seem too deep to navigate alone.

Your healing is not a destination; it is a journey and a lifelong relationship with yourself. And when you dedicate yourself to it with courage and compassion, you unlock the hidden wisdom and potential within. A focused path will lead you to greater authenticity, wholeness, and fulfillment.

The Journey Within is best navigated with structure and guidance in a space where you can integrate your healing at a sustainable pace, where you are seen, understood, validated, and held in your transformation.

Regardless of whether you are navigating your inner work alone or with guidance, these principles will make or break your transformation:

- **Trust Your Inner Guidance** — Pay attention to the recurring emotions, thoughts, and memories that surface. These are not random; they are signposts guiding you toward the shadow aspects that need exploration. While surrounding yourself with supportive individuals and communities is invaluable, the most crucial validation comes from within. You are your own greatest authority—trust yourself.

- **Trust the Process** — Shadow work is not about rushing to a finish line but about allowing yourself to unfold, process, and integrate at your own pace. Meet your shadows without judgment, hold space for discomfort, and give yourself permission to evolve organically. Transformation happens in layers—surrender to the journey rather than resisting it.

- **Strategize Cultivation** — Insight alone is not enough; true transformation happens through embodiment and action. Develop a real-life action plan for integrating the wisdom you gain into your daily life. Whether through rituals, habits, self-care practices, or conscious decision-making, create a sustainable path that supports your growth.

- **Embrace the New You** — As you shed old patterns and step into a more authentic version of yourself, honor and celebrate your transformation. Every breakthrough, no matter how small, is a victory. You are rising into greater awareness, self-empowerment, and liberation—own it.

- **Continue Growing —** Shadow work is not a one-time event; it is a lifelong journey of self-mastery. With each cycle, you will uncover new layers, deepen your self-awareness, and expand your capacity for love, compassion, and authenticity. Approach this journey with patience, persistence, and radical self-love, knowing that every step forward is a step toward your highest self.

This is your sacred becoming. Keep going!

SECTION 24. ANCHORING YOURSELF

The key to stability in transformation is anchoring.

No wonder I chose *Anchor* as the name for our shadow work grounding bracelet—it's quite fitting. Healing and transformation require grounding and unwavering focus—energetically, mentally, and emotionally. Without this balancing energy, it's easy to slip back into old patterns and feelings of uncertainty.

To anchor yourself means creating a foundation of stability as you move through deep inner work. It's about integrating the insights you gain rather than letting them drift away. Transformation is inherently destabilizing; as you shed old layers and step into your authenticity, you release conditioned responses and outdated beliefs. This process can feel overwhelming or isolating—making anchoring essential.

We'll soon circle back to the Alchemy process and explore the next *Journey Within* doorway—**The Bridge**, positioned as the transition between Fermentation and Coagulation. This is where the old dissolves and the new begins to take form. Anchoring is critical here—this is where integration happens, vulnerability shows up, and resilience is built.

As the new you materializes, not everyone can cross this bridge with you. The old must be released to welcome the new. Your past self no longer exists, and not everyone deserves access to your new energy, blessings, or light. This transformation may trigger internal and external resistance—whether from your own ego or from others clinging to who you used to be.

Anchoring practices keep you centered during this evolution. Some methods are immediate and effortless, like deep breathing or placing your hand over your heart. Others require deeper intention, such as daily rituals, movement, meditation, or journaling. The key is to find what resonates with you—what keeps you grounded, aligned, and empowered as you step into your highest self.

Consider journaling as a powerful anchor in your shadow work—yes, you read that right: *journaling!* It sounds like such a simple, no-brainer task, yet it is profoundly effective. Journaling helps you process emotions, release resistance, and stay present through transformation. Writing becomes a tool for self-reflection, allowing you to witness your thoughts, voice your feelings, and bring subconscious patterns to light.

When shadow work feels overwhelming, journaling serves as a lifeline—offering clarity and emotional regulation. It creates space for deep introspection, ensuring you remain grounded and intentional rather than lost in emotional turbulence.

To support your practice, our One Vessel membership's free tier, **Notion**, offers self-love-focused daily journaling prompts—making self-reflection accessible and easeful. Whether you're new to journaling or already practicing, these prompts guide you in exploring your shadows with depth and self-compassion.

For those who integrate tarot into their practice, **The Lantern Tarot Oracle** is crafted for illuminating introspection—helping you clarify the energy of the day and identify shadow aspects ready for healing.

JOURNEY WITHIN: DYNAMICS OF SHADOW WORK

For deeper insight, pair your daily Tarot card pull with our **Tarot for Self-Mastery Manual**, which explores the light and shadow aspects of each card. This approach transforms your tarot practice from passive card-pulling into an active process of self-awareness, growth, and empowerment.

Journaling isn't just about writing—it's a sacred ritual of self-honoring.

A practice that fosters truth, clarity, and commitment to your evolution. Whether you write freely, follow prompts, or use tarot as a guide, let journaling be your anchor as you navigate your journey within.

JOURNEY WITHIN DOORWAY #8:
The Bridge (Time and Space for Recalibration)

We're finally here—**The Bridge**.

I am especially excited about this phase because this is one of the most pivotal moments in your journey. The Bridge is where everything you've worked for takes root, where transformation shifts from concept to embodiment. You're soon to reveal as a new version of yourself. This is the threshold between who you were and who you are becoming. The way you navigate this transition determines whether your change is temporary or becomes a foundation for lasting self-mastery.

This stage is not about rushing forward—it's about integration. True healing is not a single event but a continual process of fine-tuning and realignment with your highest essence. Every recalibration strengthens your ability to hold the frequency of love, power, and purpose. Here, you allow your healed self to settle in, take root, and become an embodied reality.

At The Bridge, your newfound wisdom and transformation are put to the test. You are learning to move through life with greater confidence, trusting that your wounds have made you stronger, and your lessons have brought you closer to your authentic self. This is the space where you align your thoughts, actions, and energy with the higher version of yourself.

In Tarot storytelling, after the whole Ordeal situation, The Fool emerges from the chaos of The Tower, and enters the promise of The Star. The Tower represents upheaval, destruction, and revelation—the crumbling of false foundations, outdated beliefs, and illusions that no longer serve us. These moments, while painful, are necessary catalysts for profound transformation.

When the dust settles, The Star appears as a guiding light—a symbol of renewal, clarity, and hope. But The Star is not a finish line; it's healing in progress. The image of the Star in Tarot depicts a figure naked beneath the cosmos, fully exposed, pouring water onto the earth and into a pool—a delicate balance between grounding and emotional healing.

The Star offers the promise of renewal. It's the calm after the storm, where healing, hope, and inspiration begin to flow. This is the card of illumination, representing a clean slate and the opportunity to rebuild on a foundation of clarity and truth. But please notice the word "opportunity." While The Star brings hope and renewal, it also demands vulnerability, mindfulness, and intention to truly move forward.

This is the energy of The Bridge: vulnerable yet filled with potential. It is a sacred passage, an opportunity to integrate your transformation, align with your truth, and step forward with unwavering intention.

However, this phase comes with its own challenges. Not everyone will resonate with this new version of you—including your own ego. The remnants of your past conditioning may try to pull you back into old patterns. You may feel external resistance, internal doubt, or moments of uncertainty.

While The Star does not inherently cause sabotage, the vulnerability it brings can create subtle pitfalls, including:

- **A False Sense of Completion:** Assuming the work is done when deeper healing remains.
- **Over-Optimism:** Losing grounding by overestimating progress or bypassing necessary shadow work.
- **Dependency on External Validation:** Seeking approval or reassurance from others instead of anchoring within.

These missteps don't mean failure; they are invitations to deeper awareness and mastery.

The Bridge requires:

- **Self-awareness** to recognize subtle pitfalls like complacency, over-optimism, or dependency on validation.
- **Discernment** to filter out what no longer aligns with your highest good.
- **Boundaries** to protect your newfound frequency from anything that seeks to diminish it.

Crossing The Bridge is not just about reaching the other side—it's about claiming your evolution with confidence, purpose, and self-trust.

ILLUMINATION

Having undergone the fire of transformation and the metamorphosis of fermentation, we now arrive at The Bridge—a sacred threshold of recalibration. This is where refinement occurs, where distortions are shed, and where we align fully with our highest truth. It is a proving ground, filtering out all that no longer serves our evolution.

The Bridge teaches us discernment, boundaries, and the art of letting go. It is not merely a passage but a test of alignment, ensuring that only what resonates with our renewed frequency crosses with us. Not everyone or everything can continue forward. Some people, beliefs, and patterns will fall away—not out of cruelty, but necessity.

Why the Bridge is Crucial and Vulnerable

As we stand at this threshold, we face unique challenges that determine whether we fully integrate our transformation or remain stuck between worlds.

- **Old Shadows Resurface:** The subconscious often tests our resolve, bringing back doubts, fears, and resistance. These shadows seek validation—proof that the old version of us still exists. Without strong boundaries, it's easy to fall back into outdated roles or patterns.

- **The New Self is Still Rooting:** Like a seed breaking through the soil, our growth is real but delicate. This phase requires stability and nourishment to prevent regression. Self-care is non-negotiable—it fortifies our energy and reinforces the foundation of our becoming.

- **External Challenges Intensify:** The world may push against this shift, mirroring old expectations or questioning our evolution. Relationships may be tested. Systems that once felt comfortable may now seem restrictive. This is where we must stand firm, honoring the inner compass over external noise.

What Happens If the Bridge Isn't Crossed Properly

- **Stagnation:** Remaining in limbo, unable to fully embody transformation, leads to frustration and confusion.

- **Regression:** Without integration, old habits resurface, undoing the growth achieved through transformation.

- **Fragmentation:** A divided self emerges—one foot in the past, one in the future—causing emotional and energetic dissonance.

How to Strengthen the Bridge

- Embrace Boundaries: Protect your transformation by defining what aligns with your growth.

- Say "no" to people, habits, and environments that pull you backward.
- Honor your time, energy, and sacred space.
- Commit to Self-Care: Prioritize mind, body, and spirit nourishment. Meditation, rest, journaling, and aligned connections keep you anchored in your evolution.
- Stay Present: Rushing toward completion weakens the process. Fully experience the recalibration—reflect, feel, and adjust as needed.
- Celebrate Progress: Acknowledge each step. No matter how small, it confirms movement toward wholeness, rebirth, and divine alignment.

The Bridge as a Gateway to Mastery

This phase is both a passage and a test. It refines, recalibrates, and reaffirms who we are becoming. The Bridge ensures that only what serves our highest good moves forward. It is the final alignment before Coagulation—the embodiment of mastery, wholeness, and purpose.

Cross with intention. Cross with courage. Cross with clarity.

What's ahead? The Path.

Know Thyself: Introspections 091

91. The Bridge: What parts of my old self or life am I struggling to release, and how can I honor this transition with grace?

JOURNEY WITHIN DOORWAY #9:
The Path (The Point of No Return)

Crossing The Bridge requires courage. It is the threshold between who you were and who you are becoming—a passage that demands sacrifice, self-awareness, and unwavering commitment to your highest path.

The way backward may seem familiar, even tempting, but it only leads to the undoing of your healing and progress. There is only one true path forward.

In my personal journey, The Bridge presented profound challenges to test my devotion to self-prioritization and my divine calling. Old paradigms resurfaced and self-doubt crept in. Yet, through these trials, I learned the power of release. I let go of people and environments that no longer aligned with my energy, even when it was painful.

Temptation was present, but so was self-love. I remained steadfast in my shadow work and tarot-inspired reflections, integrating new rituals like energy work, cord-cutting, and moon intention-setting. I protected my time and energy, enforced boundaries, nurtured meaningful relationships, and dedicated myself to creative expression.

With this clarity, my needs became undeniable. I recognized my deal breakers, red flags, and non-negotiables. My boundaries evolved—not as walls but as filters, allowing only kindred, supportive energy into my life. Each decision, no matter how difficult, was a declaration of radical self-love.

On the other side of The Bridge lies The Path—a sacred trajectory illuminated by conviction and purpose. This is

INTEGRATION

where our new or renewed sense of self solidifies, and conviction takes hold. There is no turning back; once we step onto The Path, we cannot unsee or unknow the truth of who we are.

Like The Star, The Bridge is lit by clarity and hope, but that light is only a guide. Walking The Path requires conscious action, self-awareness, and unwavering dedication. Here, we align fully with our calling, stepping into the flow of our destiny.

The Path is a declaration of trust in ourselves and a devotion to our sacred mission. It urges us to channel our newfound direction into deliberate, purposeful actions that rebuild our lives in harmony with our authentic selves.

Once we walk this path, we are forever changed.

Know Thyself: Introspections 092

92. The Path: What am I certain about regarding my soul's purpose, and what steps can I take to walk this path with integrity and courage?

DOORWAY #10:
The Summit (The Cusp of Anew)

The Path leads us to The Summit, a holy altar where we are crowned in our achievement. This is where the air is clear, the weight is lifted, and we stand fully in the presence of our own evolution. Here, the veil is removed, and we see ourselves—and our journey—with divine precision. It feels like a sacred pause to catch our breath, reflect, integrate, and celebrate how far we've come.

The Summit is the space where hindsight merges with foresight, and we understand the purpose behind every challenge, sacrifice, and lesson. The trials of the past no longer weigh us down—they stand behind us as proof of our resilience. Every wound that once ached has transmuted into wisdom. Every tear, every doubt, every moment of surrender now reveals itself as necessary, shaping the being we have become.

The Summit is where you recognize yourself as the architect of your own transformation. You see the pieces that once felt scattered now forming a masterpiece. You honor not just the outcome, but every step, every misstep, every moment of perseverance that led you here.

How Do You Know You've Arrived at The Summit?

Reaching The Summit is not about external validation, nor is it about achieving perfection. It is a deeply personal realization—an unshakable inner knowing that you have transformed.

You will know you have arrived when:

- **The past no longer binds you.** You can acknowledge your history without being trapped by it. The wounds, once raw, no longer dictate your choices. Instead, they serve as reminders of how far you've come.

- **You move with certainty.** You trust yourself fully and no longer second-guess your worth, your path, or your purpose.

- **You have made peace with what was.** Resentment, regret, and resistance no longer take up space in your heart. You have forgiven—not just others, but yourself.

- **You feel light, yet strong.** The burdens you once carried have fallen away. You have reclaimed your energy and embraced the fullness of your power.

- **Your vision for the future feels aligned, not forced.** There is no longer a need to chase, prove, or force anything into being. You move in harmony with your divine path.

The Summit as a New Beginning

While The Summit offers a moment of triumph and a propelling edge, just like a launchpad where you stand at the altar of your own becoming. It's an advantage point from which new possibilities emerge. Standing here, you realize

INTEGRATION

that every peak is also a doorway—an invitation to expand further, dream bigger, and embrace the infinite nature of your evolution.

This is the sacred moment to breathe it all in. To honor yourself fully. To stand in gratitude for the journey, and to trust that the next steps will reveal themselves in divine timing.

And as you rise from this summit, remember this: you are not at the end—you are at the edge of your next becoming.

HERO'S MILESTONE 10
Receiving the Reward

In Tarot storytelling, when the Hero transcends the Ordeal, they reach a metaphorical summit and are rewarded with a Revelation. This insight could be newfound wisdom, inner strength, spiritual awakening, or the completion of a karmic cycle. The Hermit card embodies this moment.

At The Summit, we encounter The Hermit—not as a distant figure, but as a reflection of ourselves. Standing at the peak, lantern in hand, The Hermit is both the seeker and the guide, rooted in wisdom gained through solitude and sacred inner work. The lantern is not just a beacon for others, but a mirror reflecting the resilience, transformation, and self-mastery earned along the Path.

It's important to reiterate 'Arriving at the Summit' not simply a physical or external milestone—it is a shift in consciousness. It is the moment when self-doubt is replaced with inner knowing, when the noise of the world quiets, and we hear our own voice with divine precision. There is a profound sense of peace, as if all the lessons, struggles, and revelations of the journey have finally crystallized into wisdom. The burden we carried up the mountain becomes light—not because it has vanished, but because we have transformed under its weight.

Reaching The Summit is not just about arrival—it is about embodiment. The answers we seek have always been within, but it is only through stillness, introspection, and conscious action that they become clear. The Hermit reminds us that wisdom is both the reward and the responsibility of the journey. To stand at The Summit is to hold our own light with confidence, to honor the road we have traveled, and to step into the next chapter as both student and teacher.

The Hermit teaches us the profound power of self-discovery and alignment with our higher purpose. It represents a full-circle moment—from the sacred stillness of Sanctuary to the present transformation. The light we ignited within, drawn from the deepest, darkest corners of our innermost being, becomes our Revelation—a gift of wisdom and truth to be shared with others.

The Reward

In the Hero's Journey is the moment when all the trials, struggles, and transformations culminate in a significant gain—a deep, life-changing revelation. But this reward isn't always tangible. It's not just about achieving a goal; it's about becoming the person who is ready to hold and embody that wisdom, power, or transformation.

- For someone healing from past wounds, their reward might be inner peace—the moment they stop seeking external validation and finally feel whole within themselves.

- For an entrepreneur or creator, it might be clarity and confidence—a newfound certainty about their path, their voice, and their purpose.

- For a spiritual seeker, it could be alignment—the feeling of being connected to their higher self, trusting their intuition, and no longer resisting the flow of life.

- For someone working through self-sabotage, the reward is self-mastery—realizing they can break free from old cycles and reclaim their power.

How to Know You've Reached the Reward Stage

- You feel a deep sense of knowing—even if the path ahead is still uncertain, you trust yourself.

- You experience internal shifts—your triggers no longer control you, your perspective has expanded, and you respond with greater awareness.

- You feel lighter, freer, and empowered—the struggle may not be over, but you've reclaimed your sovereignty over your mind, your emotions, and your spirit.

- You realize the journey itself was the reward—because through it, you became the version of yourself who could receive and carry that wisdom.

Through my shadow work journey, I gained alignment and was propelled forward in my life's mission. My reward was healing, personal growth, and ascending into my Akasha—becoming able to be of service to you and feeling fulfilled beyond my imagination.

Shadow work was not just a path to uncovering my authentic self; it was a crucible that refined and elevated my divine purpose. I was already a healer, a teacher, and a coach, but the deep inner work sharpened my intent, focused my mission, and led to the creation of *The Journey Within* framework—the transformational process that I now offer to you through this book, its resources, and the tools of embodiment.

These tools, now available to you, helped me integrate ongoing shadow work into my self-care practice while mastering conscious detachment from toxic cords, expectations, suffering, and the illusion of control. I learned to seize, surrender, and conquer—one day at a time. This intentional, mindful process empowered me to proclaim radical self-love and activate my limitless self.

Shadow work is the ultimate act of self-love. It's candid, complex, and ongoing. And now, you have the advantage of the *Journey Within* structure and resources to make this path tangible and attainable. You also have the wisdom, love, and power within you to heal, grow, and align with your highest self. Trust that you are whole, worthy, and enough—exactly as you are. Let love guide you, and remember:

Every part of you—light and shadow—is deserving of acceptance, love, and healing.

Let's continue. The best is about to unfold.

Know Thyself: Introspections 093

93. The Summit: What have I achieved on my journey that I need to honor, and how can I celebrate my transformation?

PHASE VII
A New You

In the Hero's Journey, the final stage is the Return with the Elixir—also known as Returning Transformed- this is where the Hero returns to their world bearing the wisdom, power, or healing they gained through their trials. This is not just about coming back—it's about coming back changed and impacting the world with that transformation.

How is he transformed?

- The Hero has conquered their trials, faced death and rebirth, and emerged renewed.
- The Hero, having confronted their deepest fears and wounds, no longer rejects or suppresses aspects of themselves. Instead, they integrate their experiences, just as the World represents unity and harmony.
- The Hero is no longer just a seeker but a bringer of wisdom.
- The Hero, like the figure in the World card, understands they are part of a larger cycle, connected to all things. This is not just a personal victory but a universal realization.

In the Journey Within, this translates to embodiment and sovereignty:

- No longer seeking healing, but living as healed.

JOURNEY WITHIN: DYNAMICS OF SHADOW WORK

- No longer chasing answers, but being the answer.
- No longer denying the self, but unveiling, healing and integrating.

When people speak of a "new you," they often refer to a personal reinvention, an upgrade in consciousness, or a shift in identity. However, transformation as a result from shadow work is not about becoming someone else—it's about becoming the fullest, most realized version of yourself.

How This Plays Out in Real Life

- The "new you" after a major healing cycle—no longer react the same way, because you've integrated your past wounds. You've completed a journey of self-discovery, shadow work, or healing, and now you own all aspects of yourself—light, shadow, strengths, and lessons.
- The "new you" after stepping into purpose—no longer searching for alignment; you are aligned.
- The "new you" after mastering self-love—no longer seek validation; you embody your worth.
- The "new you" isn't about fixing something broken, but about recognizing you were whole all along. You no longer feel fragmented, uncertain, or confused, you stand in your true, unshakable essence.
- The "new you" is assertive. You've moved beyond theory and practice; now, you embody wisdom rather than just seeking it. Your transformation is no longer just internal—it radiates outward in how you live, move, and show up in the world.

DOORWAY #11:
The Vessel (The Sacred Container)

At the end of the Hero's journey, the Hero reaches a pinnacle moment of transformation, having embodied the lessons of Death, surrendered to destiny through The Wheel of Fortune, and embraced their soul's calling through Judgement. This culmination leads to the ultimate state of wholeness represented by The World, symbolizing fulfillment, self-actualization, and integration.

But this is not the end. The Hero is now reborn as the Fool 2.0—a wiser, more conscious version of themselves. This cycle reflects the natural rhythm of life: transformation is not a final destination but an ongoing process.

- The Fool represents the uninitiated, the seeker, someone stepping into the unknown with excitement but little experience.

- The World is the evolved Fool, who has walked the path, learned through trials, and emerged whole. Yet, it also hints at the next cycle—the next version of you that is ready to begin anew, this time with wisdom as your foundation rather than naivety.

The same is true for us after shadow work periods. We heal, we learn, and then we grow and evolve—again and again. Transformation is not a one-time event; it's a cyclical process that repeats throughout our lives. The version of me writing this book is not the same as the person who walked out of the ER room 10 years ago, and 10 years from now, I will have evolved once more.

The beauty of shadow work is that it doesn't just transform us passively—it makes the process conscious, intentional, and tangible. It equips us with tools to navigate the cycles of death and rebirth, helping us approach each "new version" of ourselves with clarity and empowerment.

At any age or stage, we hold the capacity to heal, to change, and to grow. What makes shadow work so profound is that it allows us to engage with this process consciously and intentionally. It turns something abstract and intangible—personal evolution—into something deliberate, empowering us to actively shape the person we are becoming.

The embodiment of your Akasha—the essence of your soul's divine blueprint—can only be realized through your authentic self. Your authentic self is the most honest and aligned version of you, free from the masks of conditioning and fear, and it is the key to manifesting your true heart's desires. Only when you embody this authenticity can you step fully into your purpose and fulfill the unique mission encoded within your Akasha.

This transformation requires the wholeness and integration symbolized by The Vessel. But what does it truly mean to be the Vessel, and how do you know when you've become it?

To be the Vessel means that you have reached a level of integration where you no longer reject, suppress, or fragment parts of yourself.

The Vessel represents your capacity to hold and honor all aspects of yourself—the light and the shadow, the lessons and the scars. It reflects your ability to carry forward the wisdom gained on your journey with grace and confidence, rather than being burdened by the weight of past experiences. Through this integration, you become not just a seeker of truth but a *carrier* of it—a living embodiment of your soul's evolution.

You, the Fool, who once stepped onto this path with curiosity and uncertainty, now emerge as the Hero of your story. Through trials, revelations, and alchemical transformations, you become the active protagonist of your journey, rewriting your narrative and taking ownership of your destiny.

You know you have become the Vessel when you no longer seek external validation to affirm your worth. When your peace is not contingent on circumstances. When you hold your own space with grace, confidence, and unwavering self-trust. You recognize that you are both student and teacher, healer and healed, creator and created—all at once.

At last, we become the Vessel—the living embodiment of our highest self. This is not about reaching a final destination where you are "complete." We are an upgraded container, flexible yet unbreakable, carrying within us limitless potential. The Vessel is both a blank canvas and a sacred space where we can hold love, compassion, and purpose without limitation.

This sacred container represents the wholeness of who we are—the integration of our experiences, healing, growth, and purpose. The Vessel calls you to fully embrace your power, purpose, and authenticity, recognizing that you are a dynamic force capable of holding and sharing your essence with the world.

Just as a vessel we are beyond capable of holding infinite potential, love, and resolve.

The Vessel also embodies the idea of carrying our Akasha, or our sacred mission, within us. It is where we fully align with our true purpose and realize our boundless potential. As we embrace this role, we become more than just individuals navigating through life—we become the active creators of our path, manifesting our deepest desires and living in accordance with our soul's mission.

This concept reflects a transition from a limited sense of self to an expanded, empowered state where we realize our capacity to hold both light and shadow and to use this integration to create a life of profound meaning and fulfillment.

HERO'S MILESTONE 11
Returning Transformed

In the Hero's Journey, The Return with the Elixir marks the final stage. The Hero, having undergone deep transformation, returns to the world—not as they were, but as a new, empowered being. The "elixir" is the wisdom, healing, and power they now possess, ready to be shared with their community. This moment signifies mastery over both inner and outer realms, aligning the self with a greater purpose.

The Ever-Evolving Vessel

The Vessel is not stagnant; it expands as you do. With each cycle of healing, learning, and growth, it stretches to hold even more of your potential. Just as the Hero's journey never truly ends, neither does your evolution.

Each healed wound, each lesson learned, opens the door to new growth. Your highest self is not a destination but a continuous unfolding—an ever-expanding vessel capable of holding both the depths of your shadow and the brilliance of your light.

One of the most profound gifts of this stage is transcending the ego. Through their journey, the Hero has dismantled illusions of separation, control, and attachment. They no longer act from fear, insecurity, or the need for validation. Instead, they:

- Act with intention and purpose.
- Stay authentic in the face of challenges.
- Embrace humility, recognizing they are part of a greater whole.
- Release attachment to outcomes, understanding their value lies in **being, not doing**.
- Serve others authentically, using their **elixir** for the collective good.
- Remain open to growth while being grounded in their values.

The Hero's return is not just for themselves. The elixir they bring back is meant to heal, inspire, and uplift others. Whether through wisdom, art, leadership, or presence, they now act as a beacon of possibility, illuminating the path for others to embark on their own transformation.

ILLUMINATION

Our version of the Fool 2.0—our Hero self—is still human. No amount of growth or transformation exempts us from sour human condition. And self-doubt is inevitable. Even as we return to the world, carrying the wisdom of our journey, we will continue to face life's trials. Evolution doesn't mean we stop questioning our worthiness or capabilities—it means we learn to move through those doubts with awareness and grace.

I know this intimately. Imposter syndrome creeps in, whispering, *Who am I to help or lead others?* I am flawed, still healing, and far from perfect. But I've come to realize that it is precisely because I am still healing that I am meant to guide. Healing is not a final destination—it is a commitment to continuous self-awareness and self-acceptance.

This upgraded vessel of myself, King Gaia, is not just a title—it is a testament. A testament to radical self-love, unfiltered shadow work, and the relentless pursuit of authenticity. Every inch of my being reflects the deep, unapologetic inner work I've done to face my wounds, and rise to my true potential. Every scar, every breakthrough, every moment of deep self-exploration has shaped me into who I am today. The King I claim to be is not born of ego but of devotion—to self-mastery, to truth, and to sacred service.

When I call myself *King*, I am not elevating myself above anyone. I am claiming, holding and occupying my space. I am standing in the fullness of my energy, my archetype, my mission. Leadership is not about perfection—it is about knowing yourself, accepting yourself, and leading from that place of wholeness. I have looked into the mirror—seen both the beauty and the pain—and chosen love. Not conditional love, but radical, unapologetic love for every part of me.

My path to this knowing was not easy. I am a masculine-presenting divine feminine, a Latina woman of color, a queer soul unapologetically standing in my truth. I am on the spectrum—highly sensitive, intuitive, and deeply attuned to the unseen. I feel more, perceive more, navigate the world through an awareness that many do not understand. But this is my gift. This is my power.

Let me be clear: I am not perfect. I have stumbled, fallen, and made mistakes. But I have chosen to rise—again and again. Not because I have it all figured out, but because I refuse to abandon or betray myself. There is no final destination. Only expansion. Only the next becoming.

This is what it means to be the Vessel. To hold both light and shadow, strength and vulnerability, wisdom and wonder. To recognize that we are always evolving, yet always whole. To understand that being the Hero of our own story doesn't mean never feeling lost—it means choosing to walk forward, even in uncertainty.

I don't need to be perfect; I need to be human.

Perfection isn't the prerequisite for leadership. *Authenticity is.* I don't need to be flawless—I need to be real. My ongoing growth allows me to lead with empathy, to connect deeply, to show others that healing is not about erasing wounds but embracing them. The Fool 2.0

understands that self-doubt is not failure—it is a sign of humility, a reminder that we are always in process.

My flaws and ongoing growth allow me to lead with empathy, understanding, and relatability. They remind me—and those I guide—that healing is a lifelong process. We don't arrive at a place where struggles vanish, but we gain tools, resilience, and self-awareness that help us navigate life with grace and wisdom.

And so, I invite you: Walk with me. Engage in the work of shadow and self-love. Do not wait until you feel "ready" or "worthy." You already are. You don't need to have it all figured out. You simply need to say *yes*—to yourself, to your journey, to your truth.

Because when you do, you will unlock a power within you that no one can take away. You will become the Hero of your own story.

E-COURSE LECTURE: "Accepting Change"

Know Thyself: Introspections 094

94. The Vessel: How can I fully embody my growth and radiate my most authentic self in my thoughts, actions, and energy?

SECTION 25. UNLOCKING YOUR SOUL'S PURPOSE (AKASHA)

The Akashic Records are often described as the energetic archive of your soul, containing all lifetimes, lessons, experiences, and contracts. However, within the context of our Journey Within progression, the Akasha refers specifically to your soul's purpose blueprint for this lifetime—a focused "file" rather than the entirety of your record. It represents the deeper "why" behind your incarnation, the lessons you are destined to learn, and the unique growth you are here to embody.

A powerful way to understand this is through astrology. The North Node serves as a visible piece of your Akasha, illuminating the soul's primary mission in this lifetime. It provides a practical and spiritual roadmap, guiding you toward the qualities, experiences, and challenges necessary for your highest evolution.

Each step in this journey brings you closer to alignment with your Akasha—your divine contract, your sacred mission. As you embody the Vessel, you activate this purpose, stepping fully into your unique power as a force of transformation in the world.

In Alchemical terms, coagulation is the final stage of transformation, symbolizing wholeness and self-mastery. You have transmuted shadow into light, integrated your experiences, and now stand as the embodiment of your soul's purpose.

To unlock your Akasha is not merely to understand your mission—it is to live it. But, how do you recognize your akasha?

Your Akasha is the energetic blueprint of your soul's purpose in this lifetime—the lessons you're here to master, the essence you're meant to embody, and the unique impact you are destined to create. Recognizing it requires deep self-awareness, alignment, and attunement to your inner truth.

Signs You Are Tapping Into Your Akasha:

A Deep, Unshakable Calling

- You feel drawn toward a path, even if it doesn't make "logical" sense.
- There's a persistent nudge or pull toward a certain mission, practice, or role in the world.
- You may have repeated synchronicities guiding you in a specific direction.

Themes & Patterns in Your Life

- Certain challenges, experiences, or lessons keep repeating—this is your soul's curriculum.
- Recurring relationships, struggles, or situations push you toward growth and mastery.
- Your childhood dreams, talents, and passions may offer clues.

Alignment Feels Like Flow

- When you step into your Akasha, there is a sense of "coming home."
- Even when challenges arise, you feel inner clarity, peace, or resilience.
- Work, creativity, or service in alignment with your Akasha feels energizing rather than draining.

A Strong Connection to Your North Node (Astrology)

- Your North Node in your birth chart highlights your soul's primary lesson in this lifetime.
- Your South Node represents past life patterns you are evolving beyond.
- Learning about your North Node's sign, house, and aspects can reveal a direct path to your Akasha.

Intuition & Inner Knowing

- When you connect with your Akasha, your intuition sharpens.
- Messages may come through meditation, dreams, or moments of deep reflection.
- You may experience downloads, sudden clarity, or a gut knowing about your path.

JOURNEY WITHIN: DYNAMICS OF SHADOW WORK

The Challenges That Shape You

- Your deepest struggles often point toward your greatest wisdom.
- The wounds you've healed hold the medicine you are meant to share.
- Facing your shadows and transmuting them into light is key to embodying your Akasha.

A Magnetic Pull Toward Service & Impact

- Your Akasha is not just for you—it's meant to be shared.
- You feel called to guide, create, teach, heal, or transform something in the world.
- The more you align with your Akasha, the more effortlessly you inspire and uplift others.

How to Deepen Your Connection to Your Akasha

- ✓ **Shadow Work** – Healing unresolved wounds clears blockages and reconnects you to your purpose.
- ✓ **Follow Your Resonance** – Reflect on what truly excites you, calls you, and refuses to let you go. Follow it.
- ✓ **Journaling & Reflection** – Ask yourself: *What themes, passions, interests, and lessons keep showing up in my life?* Honor the answers.

INTEGRATION

- ✓ **Meditation & Energy Work** – Create stillness to receive divine downloads, contemplate what's flowing through you, and gain clarity.

Your Akasha is already within you. The journey is one of remembering, aligning, and boldly stepping into your fullest expression.

Know Thyself: Introspections 095

95. The Akasha: What unique gifts or lessons have emerged from my journey, and how can I use them to fulfill my sacred mission?

ILLUMINATION
What is the North Node?

While my expertise is rooted in shadow work rather than astrology, I've found the North Node to be a transformative tool for self-discovery and alignment. It doesn't just point toward where you're going—it reveals what holds you back and what will propel you forward.

In astrology, the North Node represents your soul's mission—what you're here to learn, embrace, and embody in this lifetime. It's like a spiritual roadmap, guiding you toward a more fulfilling, authentic version of yourself.

But here's the catch: stepping into your North Node isn't easy. In fact, it often feels uncomfortable, foreign—even intimidating. That's because it requires you to break free from old patterns and step outside your comfort zone. But that discomfort? It's a sign of growth. You're on the right track! It's the feeling of expansion, of stepping into who you are meant to become.

The Push-Pull of the North & South Node

To fully understand the North Node, we have to look at its opposite: the South Node.

Your South Node represents your comfort zone—the traits, habits, and patterns you've mastered, possibly even from past lives. While these qualities feel natural, they can also hold you back if you rely on them too much. The key is to honor the strengths of your South Node while moving toward the growth of your North Node.

For example:

- South Node in Scorpio → North Node in Taurus
  You're deeply comfortable in intensity—maybe even drawn to power struggles, secrecy, or constant transformation. But your North Node is calling you to simplify, ground yourself, and find peace in stability. It's about moving away from chaos and embracing security, pleasure, and sustainability in life.

- South Node in Capricorn → North Node in Cancer
  You're used to structure, ambition, and proving your worth through achievement. But your soul's mission? Softening. Prioritizing emotional depth over external success. Learning to nurture yourself and others instead of carrying everything alone.

- South Node in Libra → North Node in Aries
  You've spent lifetimes being the peacemaker, the harmonizer, the one who puts others first. Now? Your lesson is to stand in your own power, take the lead, and embrace independence—even if it ruffles some feathers.

The North Node is more than a placement on your birth chart—it's a guide to personal evolution. When you embrace the qualities and themes of your North Node, you'll notice greater alignment in your choices and a deeper sense of purpose in your life.

How to Align with Your North Node

Living in alignment with your North Node doesn't happen overnight. It's a gradual process of growth, trial, and integration. But the more you lean into its lessons, the more life starts to feel aligned, purposeful, and expansive.

Here's how to start:

- **Awareness:** Learn the themes of your North Node and recognize where you may be resisting them.

- **Action:** Take small, conscious steps toward embodying these lessons. If your North Node calls for independence, start setting firmer boundaries. If it asks for vulnerability, have deeper conversations.

- **Courage:** Be willing to embrace discomfort. Growth isn't always easy, but it's always worth it.

Your North Node, Shadow Work & Life Mission

Shadow work and the North Node go hand in hand. Shadow work reveals what's keeping you stuck in old patterns (your South Node), while the North Node guides you toward your next evolution.

Your life mission isn't just about a single career or goal—it's about aligning your everyday life with your soul's purpose. It's how you embody the lessons of your North Node and activate the wisdom stored in your Akasha.

So ask yourself: What feels unfamiliar but exciting? What qualities do you admire in others but struggle to embrace in yourself? Chances are, that's your North Node nudging you forward.

Because at the end of the day, your highest self is already within you—your North Node simply shows you the way back home.

Know Thyself: Introspections 096-111

LIFE PURPOSE

96. Is there an inner conflict between who I am now and who I am meant to become?

97. How do the themes of my North Node shape my highest potential, and how can I integrate them into my daily life?

98. What limiting beliefs or conditioned behaviors keep me tethered to old cycles and prevent my expansion?

99. Where am I experiencing resistance, fear, or self-sabotage in stepping into my purpose?

100. What comfort zones, attachments, or fears are preventing me from embodying my highest path?

101. What unresolved shadow aspects need healing before I can fully embrace my divine calling?

102. Where do my core values and my soul's mission align, and where do they conflict?

103. What is one inspired action I can take today to embody the energy of my North Node?

104. How can I step beyond my perceived limitations to accelerate my personal and spiritual evolution?

105. How do the lessons of my past serve as fuel for my transformation and alignment with purpose?

106. What role, vocation, or creative expression feels most aligned with my passion and highest mission?

107. Does my current lifestyle and work bring me deep fulfillment, or is something essential missing?

108. How can I use my unique gifts and experiences to inspire, uplift, and connect with others?

109. What intuitive guidance, signs, or synchronicities are leading me toward my next step?

110. If I were fully living in alignment with my highest self, what would my life look and feel like?

111. What impact do I want to leave on the world, and how can I start embodying that legacy today?

SECTION 26. THE ULTIMATE OUTCOME

Shadow work is not a one-time deal; it's a lifelong unfolding, a sacred commitment to yourself. It is the work of peeling back layers, uncovering hidden truths, and reclaiming the parts of yourself that have been buried, silenced, or forgotten. This journey is not always easy, but it is always worth it.

Every insight gained, every wound healed, every step forward brings a tangible shift—not just in how you see yourself but in how you experience life. You'll notice it in the way you respond to challenges, in the way you set boundaries, in the way you speak to yourself in the quiet moments. Over time, you become lighter, freer, more *you*.

Shadow work takes you through a metamorphosis, moving from self-awareness to self-mastery. Along the way, you cultivate:

- **Self-acceptance,** embracing who you are without shame.
- **Self-compassion,** holding space for your pain while nurturing your growth.
- **Self-respect,** honoring your needs, values, and worth.
- **Self-realization,** recognizing your potential beyond fear and limitations.
- **Self-empowerment,** stepping into your truth without apology.
- **Self-actualization,** embodying the highest version of yourself.

Each of these stages is an expression of radical self-love.

But let's not forget—this isn't about reaching a final destination. There is no finish line where you "arrive" and never have to do the work again. Instead, shadow work is about integration. It's about becoming whole.

As you deepen this practice, you may experience:

- **A deep sense of self**—you truly get to know yourself.
- **A profound feeling of inner peace**—where once there was chaos, now there is clarity.
- **A life reset**—shifting from survival mode to intentional living.
- **A rebirth**—shedding outdated versions of yourself and embracing new possibilities.
- **A second chance at success and happiness**—realizing you are not bound by your past but empowered by your choices.

Your journey is personal. Your transformation is unique. While many seek individuation, authenticity, and alignment with their divine purpose, only you can define what your summit looks like.

So, ask yourself—what does freedom look like to you? What does your most empowered self feel like? How will you honor the work you've done? And how will you embrace the path ahead?

The ultimate outcome of shadow work is yours to decide. This is your story, your life, and your Journey Within. Remember that you're not alone.

You are part of a very powerful community of like-minded souls.

Feel welcome to reach out.

I am here for you, holding a brand-new lantern with your name on it...

And I can't wait to meet you.

E-COURSE LECTURE: "Co-Creator"

  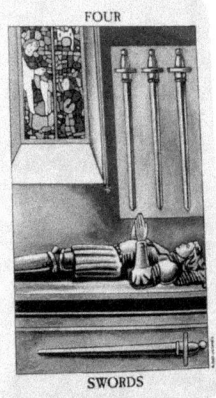

THE HEALING

- **6 of Swords** — Moving on from mental turmoil, transition.
- **8 of Cups** — Walking away from what no longer serves.
- **4 of Swords** — Rest, recovery, contemplation.

THE HEALING

- **The Hermit** — Deep introspection, inner wisdom, solitude.
- **Temperance** — Balance, alchemy, emotional healing.
- **The Hanged Man** — Surrender, new perspectives, letting go.
- **Strength** — Inner power, resilience, emotional mastery.

AFTERWORD

> **Know Thyself — A divinely guided invocation.**

Who are you today? Who will you be tomorrow? Self-discovery is not a one-time event—it's an evolving, lifelong dialogue with yourself. The 111 *Know Thyself* Self-Discovery Shadow Kit self-assessment questions woven into these pages are designed to meet you where you are, unveiling deeper layers each time you return to them.

Your answers will shift as you grow, as new insights surface, and as your awareness expands. That's the beauty of shadow work—it evolves with you.

I didn't want to just write a book; I wanted to create an experience—one that immerses you in the depths of your own being, guiding you through the intricate layers of self-awareness, healing, and transformation. The *Journey Within* Framework isn't just about reflection—it's designed to ignite, nurture, support, validate, and sustain your process. This isn't about rushing through concepts or collecting insights—it's about living them.

The introspection, the stories, the blueprint, the map—every element in this book was intentionally crafted to align with your natural rhythm of self-discovery. It unfolds in a way that allows ease, flow, and organic sequence, ensuring that each layer builds upon the last. You are not just answering questions; you are building a bridge between who you are and who you are becoming.

AFTERWORD

As you move through this journey, I encourage you to revisit this book with openness, readiness, and intention. Your responses today may differ from those six months from now because self-awareness is an ongoing process. What you resist now may be exactly what you're ready to embrace later. Shadow work isn't just about healing the past—it's about equipping yourself with the mindset to move forward.

This book is a doorway. Now, it's up to you to walk through it and keep showing up for yourself.

There was a time when I thought I had healed, only to find myself repeating old cycles. The truth is, awareness is just the beginning—commitment to change is what transforms us. My hope is that this book has given you the tools to commit to your own journey, no matter where you are on the path.

Individuation requires commitment. Awareness without action leads to stagnation, while intentional self-inquiry fuels growth. By choosing to engage with these questions, you are actively shaping your path—one that honors your truth, embraces your wholeness, and allows you to step fully into your power.

So take your time. Sit with the discomfort. Be honest with yourself. There is no rush, no right or wrong way— only the approach that aligns with where you are right now. The more you return to this work with curiosity and self-compassion, the deeper your transformation will be.

I don't expect you to embrace Tarot—but if you do, you'll find that its wisdom mirrors the very process we've explored in this book. More than a tool for insight, Tarot is an initiatory map, a catalyst for transformation, and a guide for your personal evolution.

If you're ready to integrate this wisdom into your self-mastery practice, be sure to check out my **Tarot for Self-Mastery Masterclass**. This immersive experience will equip you with everything you need to turn Tarot into an ally—one that speaks directly to your soul, offering guidance, clarity, and empowerment along the way.

And last but not least, I want you to know that presenting this material to you has been an honor and a pleasure. Witnessing how this knowledge can shift your perspective, deepen your awareness, and ultimately change your life is pure bliss to me.

Your *Fool 2.0* transformation isn't some distant possibility—it's already unfolding. Right here. Right now. Every step you take is a step toward your highest self.

Keep showing up for yourself.

ACKNOWLEDGEMENTS

This book and the entire Journey Within framework are a miracle of love—a labor of devotion, inspired action, shadow, light, and the unshakable belief in transformation.

The countless hours of research, late nights, self-contemplation revisiting my journey, insightful tarot spreads, endless cups of ginger tea, snacks, flickering candle flames, and soul-stirring background music wove together the perfect magic carpet—carrying me through the depths of introspection, revelation, and creation. I am feeling so grateful.

To my son— thank you for keeping me anchored.

To my dog—thank you for patiently sitting under my desk, wagging your tail, and keeping me company while I burned the midnight oil. You're the perfect co-worker!

To my support system—my therapist, my personal trainer, my stylist, and my barber—you keep me aligned, refined, and looking divine. This perpetual Peacock mode would not be possible without you.

To every healer, teacher, coach, guide, and wisdom keeper who has crossed my path and poured into me –your light is honored.

To my clients, students, members, followers, supporters, and customers—the soul tribe that forms this empire. I am nothing without you. Your journeys, breakthroughs, and transformations inspire me every day.

JOURNEY WITHIN: DYNAMICS OF SHADOW WORK

To the difficult upbringing that shaped my youth—thank you for the resilience, the edge, and the endless material for shadow work.

To my ancestors, seen and unseen, the otherworldly and my spirit guides who walk with me and whisper truths through the veil. —thank you for your unconditional love and protection.

To the outrageous mfrs who deliver life's most unexpected lessons—I appreciate the audacity and the golden stars I got after dealing with your f*ckery.

To divine timing, synchronicities, and universal winks that remind me I'm exactly where I need to be.

And Most Importantly, To Me:

- My inner child, the dreamer who never stopped believing, even when the world tried to convince them otherwise. Thank you for your innocence, your wonder, and your unshakable spirit.

- Former versions of myself—who has walked through fire, danced in the dark, and risen time and time again.

- My future self, the one who will look back on this moment with pride. Thank you for continuing to show up, to grow, to love, and to lead.

- And to this version of me standing here today—thank you for doing the work, for choosing yourself, for being unapologetically you. I see you. I honor you. I celebrate you. I love you.

This journey is a wild one, but damn, it's a masterpiece.

MEET THE AUTHOR

How About a Cup of Tea?

Hi there, and thank you once again for making this book a part of your personal development toolkit. I stand here before you as King Gaia, holding a lantern as bright as my intention—to be of service, to illuminate, and to walk beside you on your journey toward self-mastery.

I am a metaphysical teacher, Reiki alchemist, and shadow work coach, gracefully navigating this magical Starseed incarnation as a (queer) masculine-presenting divine feminine. My mission? Helping you connect with your most authentic self and sacred calling. I created a step-by-step **shadow work framework** designed to

guide heart-centered individuals toward radical self-love, authentic-self activation, and divine purpose fulfillment.

Through One Vessel, my sacred community, I hold space for honest self-assessment, path redesign, and sustainable personal growth. It's a safe, confidential, and non-judgmental environment for those ready to reclaim themselves.

I live and breathe self-awareness, authenticity, personal agency, and self-governance. A lover of metaphysical arts, holistic entrepreneurship, gender-neutral fashion, travel, and deep cultural immersions, I'm here to explore, expand, and empower.

Existing on the autistic spectrum keeps me humble, intuitive, and deeply attuned to the necessity of self-love, self-care, and alignment with our most authentic energy. My spiritual coaching practice is devoted to shadow work—guiding, illuminating, healing, and uplifting souls toward self-actualization. I believe in the power of radical self-acceptance, and I'm honored to walk this path alongside you.

If you're reading this, know that you matter. Your energy, your presence, your voice, your message, and your legacy are all important. Your journey within matters. Whether I serve as an inspiration, a steppingstone, a mirror to your potential, or a timely reminder of your divinity—I'm grateful to be here with you.

Email me, grab my social links, or join me at a networking event near you.

And if you ever feel called to chat over a cup of tea—Live on Instagram or YouTube—just know: I'm always down.

Once again, thank you for your support and for the opportunity to be of service to you.

I am truly grateful for you, and I can't wait to meet you.

A Special Invitation

In Tarot storytelling, The Magician holds all the tools needed for mastery, and in our *Journey Within*, as we access our innermost, these Magician tools become enchanted keys for transformation.

The wand, the cup, the sword, the pentacle. These are not just symbols. They are reflections of our mind, heart, voice, and power. The wand of willpower, the cup of emotion, the sword of truth, and the pentacle of embodiment—each one is already within us, awaiting activation.

We are called to remember: **We already possess the tools**. The Magician is not a trickster of illusions, but a divine alchemist, the mystic, the sacred co-creator within, and the one who weaves the invisible into the tangible through presence, intention, authenticity, and will.

Yet, for many, these tools remain buried beneath the rubble of unprocessed pain, hidden traumas, inherited wounds, self-limiting patterns and fractured self-worth.

Shadow work is the sacred art of uncovering them. It is the inner alchemy—not for spectacle or ego, but for soul reclamation. It's how the unseen becomes seen, how our pain becomes power, how you heal, transmute, ascend and how the fractured becomes whole. Every shadow held in compassion becomes fuel for magic. Every lie unlearned becomes a spell broken. Every truth reclaimed becomes a new powerful spell cast in your favor.

The Magician is not a role we perform. It's a state of consciousness we remember. And if you are ready to awaken the Magician within... If you are called to reclaim your sacred tools... If you are devoted to turning your shadows into spells of power...

Join me inside One Vessel—a guided journey of radical self-love, authentic self-cultivation, limitless-self activation, and divine purpose alignment.

One of the most frequently asked questions I receive is **"Where do I start?"**

Whether it's about the right order of the *Journey Within* framework, which product to use first, or what session to book—it all centers around how to begin.

The truth is, I believe Spirit always leads you to my door in divine timing, using the exact right tool, in alignment with your vibrational state and readiness.

Some of you are first drawn to my candle. Others discover my Tarot oracle deck, or find this book in your hands when you need it most. You may meet me through a YouTube video, a Tarot class, or in person—at a live event. And must likely, if you purchased any of my products, Spirit handed you a key. Literally. The key to unlocking your true heart's desires.

I could say...

- My book and teachings educate
- Sanctuary reveals and helps release
- Energy Leadership sessions illuminate and initiate
- Sacred Jewelry grounds and protects
- And One Vessel cultivates and deepens

No matter the gateway—you're guided to **shadow work**.

Because you are ready and worthy. Ready to embody the most authentic version of yourself. And worthy of fulfillment.

You're invited to upgrade your vessel and awaken the mystic, alchemist, or sacred co-creator within you. And you cannot truly achieve that state if you don't know your tools. If you can't recognize or access your power or stand firmly in your own divinity.

Shadow work is what makes that possible.

I chose to name our collective offering One Vessel very intentionally. The Vessel is you… the sacred embodiment of your authentic self. A living divine archetype capable of manifesting your true desires and alchemizing your lived experience into sacred purpose.

So, wherever you begin your shadow work, trust that you've already started on divine timing. And you're not alone. We are here to walk with you, every step of the way.

One Vessel is weekly spiritual life coaching and guided shadow work sanctuary centered on radical self-love, limitless-self activation, authentic-self cultivation and divine purpose alignment. But in essence—One Vessel is so much more than a program.

We are a spirit-led community of like-minded souls walking the path of becoming.

We are united by purpose. We show up, for ourselves and each other, devoted to healing, rising, and reclaiming our wholeness. Together, we uncover and dismantle barriers to self-love, making space for healing and personal transformation.

Inside One Vessel, I offer

- Self-paced online sessions and cultivation worksheets.
- Safe and compassionate guidance on how to take, hold, and occupy sacred space—making room for healing, clarity, empowerment, and transformation.
- Monthly live Q&A sessions to expand on topics and collective energy leadership sessions.
- Flexible membership tiers, including a 100% free level—not a trial, but a real, consistent offering.

This is your invitation, beloved.
The portal is open. Through the One Vessel path, we don't just hold the tools—we become the vessel that channels them.

WWW.KINGGAIA.COM/ONEVESSEL

www.ingramcontent.com/pod-product-compliance
Lightning Source LLC
Chambersburg PA
CBHW071812230426
43670CB00013B/2431